Sound

Scriptural

Sermon

Outlines

NO. 3

By Wade H. Horton

Limp ISB 0-87148-780-2
Hardback ISB 0-87148-781-0

Printed in the United States of America

SOUND SCRIPTURAL SERMON OUTLINES

Number 3

This outline book has been prepared with prayer and a compassionate desire that it will be helpful to fellow ministers, and most especially the young inexperienced ones. Generally, they are neither hesitant nor embarrassed to seek sermonic material from available sources.

These sermon outlines have been gathered and prepared over the years. They were selected out of a great stack of materials, some typewritten, others were notes scribbled by pen or pencil during the times I had no secretary. Some of them have been used often by this preacher, others (two or three) though outlined well, were laid aside because after their preparation there was no leading or desire to preach them. It will be easy for any God-called preacher to understand this reasoning. They have come (1) out of my own prayer and study, (2) from hearing other preachers in church, on radio and other places, (3) and from a storehouse of good books and religious materials on the shelves of my study.

It would be impossible to give credits because of not keeping records on the subject matter gathered from so many sources, and at so many different times during the forty-four years of my preaching ministry.

The writer has no hesitancy, however, in acknowledging that some of the materials in this book are not original. Much thanks and appreciation is due to a congenial and competent secretary, Mrs. Selma Siler Swindell. May God bless her and reward her for her kind assistance in typing and arranging this material for publication.

This outline book, entitled SOUND SCRIPTURAL SERMON OUTLINES, is therefore sent on its way with another prayer and with many others to follow that the sermons will be satisfactory to ministers, edifying to the church and glorifying to God, our heavenly Father. May the Holy Ghost accompany each of the sermons and anoint every preacher that uses them. This is asked in the precious Name of Jesus Christ, my Saviour and Lord.

WADE H. HORTON

PREFACE

In a special resolution of appreciation extended to the Reverend Dr. Wade H. Horton by his denomination, it was stated, "through example as a Christian, minister, and general church leader, and through dynamic preaching and teaching, and writings, he has strongly emphasized the principles of holiness to the Church and strongly urged adherence to them."

Wade H. Horton is revered as a spiritual giant among Christian believers. His fervent preaching and defense of the gospel has been eloquent, forceful, and consistent. It is especially fitting, therefore, that he offer to his contemporaries an additional volume of his sermons.

Brother Horton, as he is affectionately known to thousands, has been a preacher for forty-five years. During his long and impressive ministry, he has pastored some of the most prestigious churches in his denomination. He served as state overseer of Mississippi and South Carolina, and he was the Foreign Missions Field Representative for six years.

Except for two years, Dr. Horton has served on the Executive Council of his church, either by election or by virtue of his executive office, since 1953. He has served for a total of fourteen years on the Executive Committee of the Church of God. He was the General Overseer, the highest executive officer, from 1962-66 and from 1974-76.

During his illustrious ministry, the Reverend Horton has traveled in 103 countries. A powerful speaker, Brother Horton has preached in many of the great religious convocations around the world. Among the seven books he has authored previously are *Pentecost: Yesterday and Today, Trinitarian Concept of God, Unto the Uttermost* and *The Seven Golden Candlesticks.*

This eighth book from Dr. Horton's pen is the third in a series titled *Sound Scriptural Sermons*. The reader will find the sermons to be especially helpful. Obviously prepared under the unction of God, refined through the process of having been preached and proved by the marvelous results they have received, these messages deserve wide reading. They will offer direction, consolation, and nurture to the average reader. The minister will find them to be studied, Biblical and preachable!

It is a personal pleasure to commend these sermons to you. They come from the mind and heart of one of the truly significant preachers and leaders of our time. He is a good friend, an esteemed colleague, and a dear brother in Christ.

Cecil B. Knight

CONTENTS

Behold the Lamb of God

John 1:29

INTRODUCTION: John was the forerunner who was sent before Christ and was just a "voice of one crying in the wilderness, Prepare ye the way of the Lord, make his paths straight. Matt. 3:3. He spoke the most wonderful words, ". . . Behold the Lamb of God, which taketh away the sin of the world." John 1:29. The lamb is the emblem of—

I. INNOCENCY

A. Jesus was entirely innocent. He had no guilt nor guile.

B. But He took our guilt and therefore became guilty.

C. His nature was spotless, His life was perfect, His conduct unblamable. 1 Peter 1:19.

D. He had not one sinful weakness or infirmity. "Who did no sin, neither was guile found. . . ." 1 Peter 2:22.

II. MEEKNESS AND PATIENCE

A. They railed on Him, despised Him, mocked Him and insulted Him.

B. ". . . endured such contradiction of sinners against himself. . . ." Heb. 12:3.

C. "He is brought as a lamb to the slaughter." Isa. 53:7.

D. Before the priests, Pilate, Herod and on the cross He exemplified the meekness and patience of a lamb.

III. USEFULNESS

A. There is no creature more useful than the lamb. Meat for food—wool for raiment.

B. Jesus says, ". . . my flesh is meat indeed, and my blood is drink indeed." John 6:55. ". . . "Except ye eat the flesh of the Son of man, and. . . ." V. 53.

C. Christ provides for us the best robe, the wedding garment and the garment of salvation.

D. Flesh for spiritual food, strength, health, etc. Raiment for comfort and protection.

IV. JESUS IS THE LAMB OF GOD

A. He is the only begotten of the Father; His essential co-equal. John 1:14. Yet He is the sacrifice of God to a lost world, the Lamb of God. John 1:29.

B. The love offering of the Father to a sin-infested world. John 3:16.

C. His work is to take "away the sin of the world." John 1:29. How? By sacrifice of Himself.

1. *BY HIS OBEDIENCE AND DEATH HE TOOK AWAY THE CURSE OF SIN FROM THE WORLD.*

   a. The whole world was guilty, wrecked, helpless and condemned. *Death was the penalty.* Rom. 6:23.

   b. He ". . . gave himself for us." Titus 2:14.

   c. ". . . redeemed us to God by thy blood." Rev. 5:9.

   d. ". . . he appeared to put away sin by the sacrifice of himself." Heb. 9:26. ". . . he was manifested to take away our sins." 1 John 3:5.

2. *HE TAKES AWAY GUILT OF SIN BY HIS JUSTIFYING GRACE*

   a. Titus 2:11-13: "For the grace of God that. . . ."

8

b. Rom. 5:1: "Therefore being justified by faith, we have peace with God, through. . . ."

3. *HE TAKES AWAY THE POLLUTION OF SIN BY HIS SPIRIT AND BLOOD.*

   a. His Spirit applies the blood, thus cleansing us from all sin.

   b. Sanctified by the blood. Heb. 13:12: ". . . that he might sanctify the people with his own blood. . . ." "For both he that sanctifieth and they who are sanctified are all of one: for which cause he is not ashamed to call them brethren." Heb. 2:11.

Let's look at THE ATTENTION CHRIST DEMANDS! Behold! Look! We can't see Him as the people in those days. He is now in the holy place in heaven.

V. BEHOLD HIM IN THE MYSTERY OF HIS INCARNATION

   A. How that even though He was God, the Son, ". . . he humbled himself, and became obedient unto death, even the death of the cross." He stooped low to save the lost.

   B. He was conceived by the Holy Ghost and born of woman. A wedding of humanity and divinity. Luke 1:28-35.

   C. ". . . though he was rich, yet for your sakes he became poor, that ye through his poverty might be rich." 2 Cor. 8:9.

VI. BEHOLD HIM IN HIS SPOTLESS LIFE

   A. He was holy, undefiled.

   B. Don't look at the failure of professing Christians, look at Jesus, pure and spotless. 1 Peter

9

1:19: ". . . lamb without blemish and without spot."

VII. BEHOLD HIM IN THE OVERWHELMING AGONIES OF GETHSEMANE

A. Giving His soul an offering for sin.

B. Drinking the bitter cup.

C. "Father, let this cup pass from me."

VIII. BEHOLD HIM IN HIS SUFFERING ON THE CROSS

A. He was forced to Calvary's summit and crucified between two thieves.

B. Dying amid darkness of the heavens, shaking earth, bursting rocks.

C. He suffered like no other man and He did it all for sinful humanity.

IX. BEHOLD HIM IN HIS RESURRECTION

A. He was once dead, but alive again. Rev. 1:18: "I am he that liveth, and was dead; and, behold, I am alive for evermore. . . ."

B. He said, ". . . I am the resurrection, and the life. . . ." John 11:25, 26.

C. No man could really take his life. He laid it down for us.

X. BEHOLD HIM AS MEDIATOR ON THE THRONE

A. His toil changed to rest, His suffering to glory, His cross to the throne and crown. He is presently making intercession for us. ". . . He is able also to save them to the uttermost . . . seeing he ever liveth to make intercession for them." Heb. 7:25.

10

XI. WE SHOULD BEHOLD HIM WITH REVERENCE AND HUMILITY

We should bow down before Him and worship Him. Psalm 95:6.

Angels and all the hosts of heaven worship Him.

Behold Him with shame and contrition. Isa. 53:5: "He was wounded for our transgressions, he was. . . ." "They shall look upon me whom they have pierced." Zech. 12:10.

XII. BEHOLD HIM WITH EYE OF FAITH

"Look unto me, and be ye saved. . . ." Isa. 45:22.

". . . if I be lifted up . . . [I] will draw all men unto me." John 12:32.

"All that . . . come to me . . . I will in no wise cast out." John 6:37.

CONCLUSION: "If we confess our sins, he is faithful and just to forgive us our sins, and. . . ." 1 John 1:9.

What Do You Have in Your Hand?

Ex. 4:2

INTRODUCTION: This message should be an encouragement and a challenge. Moses made excuses, but God shows him what can be done by obedience to Him.

I. MOSES HAD A ROD AND IT BECAME A WAND.

   A. The rod he used as a shepherd is so blessed of the Lord that it becomes a mighty force in his hand.

   B. The results of using the rod is:
      1. miracles were wrought.
      2. king shaken on his throne.
      3. God's people delivered.

II. DAVID HAD A SLING AND HE USED IT TO SLAY A GIANT.

   A. He could not use Saul's armour. 1 Sam. 17:40.

   B. Smallest (?) brought down the largest.

   C. God helped him use what he had.

   D. We are in battle today. The army of the devil is challenging the army of the Lord. What is in your hand?

III. GIDEON USED TRUMPET, LAMP AND PITCHERS.

   A. It was a peculiar battle and peculiar weapons. Judges 7.

   B. God takes foolish things to confound the wise. 1 Cor. 1:27-29.

   C. Great preacher prepared a great sermon to preach to a great man. It rained. God told him to go to his house. He witnessed to him and won him to the Lord.

IV. SAMSON USED THE JAWBONE OF AN ASS. Judg. 15:15

A. Such a small thing to fight with against so many.

B. But the Spirit of God came on him.

C. The thing you have (your talent) might put a thousand to flight.

D. Try it. If God is with you, all things are possible.

V. A WOMAN HAD A HANDFUL OF MEAL. 1 Kings 17:13

A. She gave part to the prophet of God.

B. It was a great sacrifice.

C. God was depending on her to sustain His preacher.

D. Some say the preacher should work on a secular job. A good preacher's time is well taken on one job.

VI. A JEWISH MAID HAD A FEEBLE VOICE, BUT USED IT TO TELL A GREAT MAN ABOUT GOD. 2 Kings 5:1-4

A. Her testimony caused Naaman to be healed.

B. Anybody can win someone.

C. The Christian is a witness. Acts 1:8.

D. It is not an optional obligation. It is a must.

VII. THE WIDOW HAD TWO MITES. Luke 21:1, 4

A. Millions had been inspired by her giving.

B. Smallest coin.

C. Jesus saw the rich give their offerings and He saw the widow make her sacrifice.

D. One preacher said that "God does not judge a man according to what he gives, but according to what is left in his pocket."

E. The poor widow made a great sacrifice. The rich made no sacrifice.
One man said, "Give not from the top of your purse, but from the bottom of your heart."

"It's not what you would do with a million,
If riches should e'er be your lot;
But what are you doing at present
With the dollar and a quarter you've got?"

Selected

VIII. THE LAD WITH FIVE LOAVES AND TWO FISHES. John 6:9

A. This seemed small to such a large crowd.

B. It was a great sacrifice to the lad. It was probably his lunch.

C. He got back more in return and also saw a great miracle.

D. "Give, and it shall be given unto you." Luke 6:38.

IX. MARY HAD A BOX OF OINTMENT. John 12:3

A. She had a great love for Jesus.

B. The ointment was very costly.

C. She anointed his feet and wiped them with her hair.

D. The house was filled with the odor.

E. She blessed Jesus by her sacrifice, and blessed others.

14

F. Faultfinding Judas, verses 4-6. One or more in every crowd and in every church.

X. DORCAS HAD A NEEDLE. Acts 9:36, 39.

A. Dorcas was a willing worker.

B. The widows were weeping and showing the garments Dorcas had made for them. This showed her great service and influence.

C. This was a memorial forever to Dorcas.

D. It pays to be faithful. Rev. 2:10.

E. Any woman can do this much if she so desires.

CONCLUSION: What do you have in your hand? Everybody has something! The question is, Will you use it for God's glory? You can either sing in the choir—pray in the altar—pray in secret for the pastor and church—give testimony in church, in the shop, in the factory, store or office. Do you have tithes in your hand? Your tithes help the church, the pastor, yourself and the extension of the church's service and influence. Use what you have!

Four Nevers

John 11:23-26

INTRODUCTION: These four nevers are great guarantees to the believer. Those who follow Jesus Christ have the greatest assurance in the world.

I. NEVER THIRST John 4:14

A. "But whosoever drinketh of the water that I shall give him shall never thirst; but the water that I shall give him shall be in him a well of water springing up into everlasting life."

B. Wells of this world will go dry. They are "broken cisterns." Jer. 2:13.

C. Waters of salvation never run dry. ". . . the river of God, which is full of water." Psa. 65:9. Always springing up. Always an abundant supply. John 7:37-39.

II. NEVER HUNGER John 6:35

A. Jesus said unto them, "I am the bread of life: he that cometh to me shall never hunger."

B. Shortage of bread many times in the history of mankind.

C. This bread (Jesus) is never rationed.

D. "In the days of famine they shall be satisfied." Psa. 37:19.

III. NEVER PERISH John 10:27, 28

A. "My sheep hear my voice, and I know them, and they follow me: And I give unto them eternal life; and they *shall never perish*."

B. If we continue to follow him we will not perish. 1 John 2:6.

C. He gives eternal life if we follow.

D. We shall never perish if we love Him and keep His commandments. John 14:15, 23.

E. What an assurance. There is no fear of the future.

IV. NEVER SEE DEATH John 8:51

A. "If a man keep my saying, he shall never see death."

B. Romans 5:12 tells us that by one man's sin, death passed upon all men. Natural or physical death.

C. But *never see death* means the second death. Rev. 20:14. It is appointed unto man once to die. Heb. 9:27.

D. Rom. 6:23: "For the wages of sin is death; *but the gift of God* is eternal life." The greatest gift, the gift of God is eternal life.

CONCLUSION. To serve Christ means never thirst, never hunger, never perish, never see death.

The Trial of Abraham

Gen. 22:1, 2

INTRODUCTION: The word "tempt" properly signifies to test, to try or to prove.

The scene before us was intended to try the greatness of Abraham's love to, and faith in, God. He had been tried before, but here he is *subjected to the severest sacrifice ever made by man.*

Three things are presented:
    (1) The command of God.
    (2) The obedience of Abraham.
    (3) The final results.

I. THE COMMAND OF GOD

"Take now thy son . . . and. . . ."

    A. The Object Referred to: thy Son!
        Did you hear that Abraham? "Thy son!" It is not a bullock, nor rams; not even a servant, *BUT THY SON.*

        It is thine only son, Isaac. It is not Ishmael, the son of the bondswoman, *but Isaac, the son of Sara the son of promise.*

    B. The Duty Enjoined.
        1. He was commanded to "offer him as a burnt-offering."

        2. God said, "take away his life with your own hand."

    C. The Difficulties Connected With This Command.
        1. It was strange and unprecedented. Nothing like it had ever come out of the mouth of the Lord before.

        2. The sacrifices of beasts commanded before,

but human sacrifice . . . never in the history of man.

a. *It was a violation of divine law.* Gen. 9:6: "Whoso sheddeth man's blood, by man shall his blood be shed: for in the image of God made he man."

b. *He is telling him to do what He has already said not do!* It is stunning, shocking and yes, unbelievable!

c. *It would annihilate all hopes he had in his promised seed.*

   (1) God had promised him that through Isaac, should all nations be blessed.

   (2) He had long expected this fulfillment. He had prayed for it, BUT NOW— what a change!

d. *It would destroy all his domestic comfort!*

   (1) How would Sarah, his wife, bear these tidings? From the hour Isaac died, there would be darkness, gloom and despair in his home.

   (2) *Life would be unbearable to him.* It would be hard to ever have a happy home again.

e. *It would make him odious and obnoxious to all around him.*

   (1) How would he clear his character?

   (2) How could he wash his son's blood off his hands?

   (3) How could he defend his actions? If he said, "God told me!" who would believe it? They could point to Gen. 9:6.

II. THE OBEDIENCE OF ABRAHAM

A. He Was Prompt.

   Abraham rose up early. He did not hesitate. He sought no delay and required no time for con-

19

sideration. "To obey is better than sacrifice."
1 Sam. 15:22.

B. It Was Deliberate.
Whatever anguish he may have felt within, there
was no confusion in his manner. There was no
shunning and no complaining his lot. He gets his
servants ready and the wood prepared, the ani-
mals saddled and he starts on the journey. "He
staggered not at the promise of God through unbelief, but was strong in faith. . . ." Rom. 4:20.

C. It Was Persevering.
1. The journey was three days length. During
   all the long journey, Isaac was before his eyes.
2. There was plenty of time for doubt. Plenty of
   time to back out.
3. Besides, there was Isaac's distressing question. "Behold the fire and the wood: but
   where is the lamb"? Isaac's searching eyes, his
   questioning look was always upon him.
4. There was pain in his heart, but the confusion
   of mind didn't hinder him in obeying God.

III. THE FINAL RESULTS

A. Isaac Is Spared.
An angel of the Lord called, "Abraham, Abraham [twice] . . . Lay not thine hand upon the
lad." *Isaac was given back from the dead.* Heb.
11:17, 19.

B. A Sacrifice Provided.
1. Abraham looked and saw a ram caught in a
   thicket (v. 13). Of course, God caught the ram.
2. Abraham's answer to Isaac. The promise, "God
   will provide . . ." (v. 8) was fulfilled.

C. Abraham Was Commended for His Faith and
Love to God.

20

The Lord said, "because thou hast done this thing, and hast not withheld thy son, thine only son . . . I will bless thee. . . ." VV. 16, 17.

D. The Promise Is Renewed.

"In blessing I will bless thee, and in multiplying I will multiply thy seed as the stars of the heaven, and as the sand which is upon the sea shore; and thy seed shall possess the gate of his enemies."

APPLICATION:

(1) The "nature" of true acceptable obedience is to do whatever God commands.

(2) The "principle" of true obedience is faith in God.

(3) The "power" of faith is the sacrifice it freely makes.

CONCLUSION: The reward of true obedience, Abraham (1) heard God's promise again, (2) he stood the supreme test, (3) he got his son back, and (4) he witnessed the power of faith.

Immovable Saints

Psa. 62:2, 6

INTRODUCTION: Referring to the physical sufferings of one of his missionary brethren, one minister wrote that the burden, "may look to some outsiders like a tombstone hung around his neck, but in reality it was only a weight necessary to keep down the diver while he was collecting pearls."

Afflictions are weights, yet they are not sent to crush us, but only to enable us to gather the precious pearls of divine truth, and add to our rich store of Christian joy.

David was a man of afflictions, yet he learned many precious truths and passed them on to us. There are four divisions of this Psalm: (1) He speaks to his enemies. (2) Then to himself, 5-7. (3) To his friends, 8-11. (4) Then to the Lord, 12. As he thought about his enemies he didn't feel sure of himself so he said, ". . . I shall not be greatly moved." He was "afraid" not to serve. Then he shouts, "I shall not be moved." There is only one word different between the two statements. But what a difference. He got his mind off his enemies and thought about God. "My soul, wait thou only upon God; for my expectation is from him." V. 5. Some think we must be moved a little. "He only is my rock and my salvation: he is my defence," said David. V. 6.

I. SATAN SEEKS TO MOVE US. 2 Sam. 24:1.

    A. "And again the anger of the Lord was kindled against Israel, and he [Satan] moved David against them to say, Go, number Israel and Judah." He ordered Joab to number them.

    B. David's heart smote him. "I have sinned," he declared.

    C. The devil is forever trying to move us to disobey

God. What chance have we against this great
deceiver? 1 Pet. 5:8; James 4:7.

D. "For the king trusteth in the Lord, and through
the mercy of the most High he shall not be
moved." Psa. 21:7.

II. SIN SEEKS TO MOVE US.

A. Joseph's brothers were "moved with envy"
when they sold him. Acts 7:9.

B. Sin can get such a hold on us until we will be
moved with envy or jealousy.

C. Sin separates us from God. Isa. 59:2.

D. ". . . sin, when it is finished, bringeth forth
death." James 1:15.

III. AFFLICTIONS SEEK TO MOVE US.

A. Paul sent Timothy to visit the church at Thessa-
lonica lest any of them should be moved by afflictions. 1 Thess. 3:3.

B. They were having a tough time because of their
persecutions and sorrows.

C. Troubles, trials, persecutions try to move all of
us.

D. "Cast thy burden upon the Lord, and he shall
sustain thee: he shall never suffer the righteous
to be moved." Psa. 55:22.

E. "Many are the afflictions of the righteous: but
the Lord. . . ." Psa. 34:19. "But the Lord . . ."
makes the difference.

IV. FRIENDS SOMETIMES SEEK TO MOVE US.

A. Paul, believing himself to be in the will of God,
was on his way to Jerusalem, but friends tried
to dissuade him. He declared, "But none of
these things move me. . . ." Acts 20:24.

B. Many times friends who mean well advise us wrong. If you listen to friends and loved ones instead of God you will soon be moved.

C. One man was told, "The whole world is against you." He replied, "Then, I am against the whole world."

D. "Be not moved away from the hope of the gospel. . . ." Col. 1:23.

E. 1 Cor. 15:58: "Be ye stedfast, unmoveable, always abounding. . . ."

F. Psa. 15:5: "He that doeth these things shall never be moved." What things? (Verses 2-4.)

G. 2 Pet. 1:10: "If ye do these things, ye shall never fall. . . ." What things? "Add to your faith virtue; and to virtue knowledge; And to knowledge temperance; and to temperance patience; and to patience godliness; And to godliness brotherly kindness; and to brotherly kindness chairty. VV. 5-7.

CONCLUSION: Nations are being moved, so are politicians, churches and individuals. But by the grace of God I shall not be moved.

Risen With Christ

Col. 3:1-17

INTRODUCTION: This Scripture speaks about a spiritual resurrection. A resurrection in this life. There must be a death and burial before a resurrection. Verse 3 states, "Ye are dead. . . ." Gal. 2:20: "I am crucified. . . ." Rom. 6:3: "Know ye not, that so many of us as were baptized into Jesus Christ were baptized into his death?" Romans 6:6: "Knowing this, that our old man is crucified with him. . . ." Eph. 2:1: ". . . Were dead in trespasses and sins." We are now dead to sin and crucified with Christ. ". . . nevertheless I live. . . ." Gal. 2:20.

I. THE RISEN LIFE IS A LIFE OF PUTTING OFF.

   A. "But now ye also put off all these; anger, wrath, malice, blasphemy, filthy communication out of your mouth." V. 8. "Lie not one to another, seeing that ye have put off the old man with his deeds." V. 9. See Eph. 4:22-24.

   B. Like a snake shedding his skin, these must go when the old man goes. *He takes his deeds with him.*

   C. ". . . let us lay aside every weight, and the sin which. . . ." Heb. 12:1. "Having therefore these promises, dearly beloved, let us cleanse ourselves. . . . 2 Cor. 7:1.

II. IT IS A LIFE OF PUTTING ON.

   A. "And have put on the new man, which is renewed in knowledge after the image of him that created him." V. 10. "Put on therefore . . . bowels of mercies, kindness. . . ." V. 12.

   B. We cannot put on the "new man" and still retain the "deeds of the old man." They are not compatible. Both will not stay in the same house.

25

C. And above all put on charity. (V. 14).

D. "Therefore we are buried with him by baptism into death: that like as Christ was raised up from the dead by the glory of the Father, even so we also should walk in *newness of life*." Rom. 6:4.

E. "For if we have been planted together in the likeness of his death, we shall be also in the *likeness of his resurrection*." 2 Cor. 5:17; Rom. 6:5.

III. IT IS A LIFE OF SEEKING (V. 1)

A. We are not to seek earthly things, but heavenly. Seek those things which are above. V. 2.

B. Seeking heaven's approval not earthly applause.

C. *Things above* should always be attractive and appealing. We should be like Abraham, "he looked for a city which hath foundations, whose builder and maker is God." Heb. 11:10.

IV. IT IS A LIFE OF PEACE (V. 15)

A. "And let the peace of God rule in your hearts." Then there will be no sin to haunt you or trouble you.

B. When Jesus appeared to His disciples He said, ". . . Peace be unto you."

C. We have peace because the risen Christ is with us.
   1. He is the "Prince of Peace." Isa. 9:6.
   2. He wills us peace. John 14:27.
   3. It is a "peace . . . which passeth all understanding." Phil. 4:7.

V. IT IS A LIFE OF JOY AND SINGING.

A. "Teaching and admonishing one another in psalms and hymns and spiritual songs, singing with grace in your hearts to the Lord." V. 16.

B. "Be not drunk with wine, wherein is excess; but be. . . ." Eph. 5:18.

C. "Speaking to yourselves in psalms and hymns and spiritual songs, singing and making melody. . . ." V. 19.

D. The risen life is not a down in the mouth, sad, melancholy life, but a singing, shouting, rejoicing life.

E. We can sing and rejoice even in the darkest hour. Acts 16:25. Because He is no longer in the tomb. He sits in the heavenlies. Mark 16:19; Acts 7: 55, 56; Heb. 8:1, 2.

VI. IT IS A LIFE OF POWER.

A. Matt. 28:18: After the resurrection Jesus said, "All power is given unto me in heaven and in earth."

B. The world thought He was helpless, but by submitting to death He received life and power.

C. By following Christ and submitting to Him, we can receive the power of a resurrected life. Acts 1:8; Rom. 8:11.

D. The disciples returned to Jerusalem after the resurrection and went to the upper room with joy and more power. This sad, cringing, backward, humiliated group became an aggressive, stalwart and powerful group, who could *turn the world upside down.*
"Peter, standing up with the eleven. . . ." Acts 2:14. He was *standing up* unafraid of the people and not denying his Lord.

VII. IT IS A LIFE OF VICTORY.

A. He was captured by death. He was put in the tomb. The Roman seal was on it. It was guarded, but on the third day, He came out victorious!

B. "I am he that liveth, and was dead; and, behold, I am alive for evermore, Amen; and have the keys of hell and of death." Rev. 1:18.

C. ". . . thanks be to God, which giveth us the victory through our Lord Jesus Christ." 1 Cor. 15: 57.

". . . this is the victory that overcometh the world, even our faith." 1 John 5:4.

". . . we are more than conquerors through him that loved us." Rom. 8:37.

CONCLUSION: This spiritual resurrection gives real life, abundant life. It is a life the average person never experiences, but the Christian enjoys the peace and satisfaction of it every day.

What Will You Say?

Jer. 13:21

INTRODUCTION: The Word of God contains many precious promises to people who love and fear God. And contains many threatenings of future punishment to those who obey not the Gospel of Christ. The holy nature of God renders it absolutely certain that all impenitent sinners will be punished. God is asking when future punishment comes, "What wilt thou say?"

I. SOMETIMES PUNISHMENT STARTS IN THIS WORLD.

Examples: Flood—Sodom—Pharoah—Achan—Gehazi —Ananias and Sapphire—Herod—Jerusalem, etc.

II. AND SURELY THE GUILTY WILL BE AFFLICTED AFTER DEATH.

The rich man was buried and in hell lifted up his eyes. Luke 16:22, 23.

III. IT WILL BE CONSUMMATED AT THE JUDGMENT!

The body will be raised and reunited and both body and soul consigned to hell.

"And whosoever was not found written in the book of life was cast into the lake of fire." Rev. 20:15.

IV. IT WILL BE PROPORTIONATE.

Some will be beaten with few stripes. Luke 12:46-48.

Every man will be rewarded according to his works. Rev. 22:12.

"Who will render to every man according to his deeds." Rom. 2:6.

V. IT WILL BE EVERLASTING!

"Everlasting fire" Matt. 18:8; "Everlasting punishment" Matt. 25:46; "Everlasting destruction" 2 Thess. 1:9; "Everlasting chains" Jude 6; "Unquenchable fire." Matt. 3:12.

VI. BUT THE SUBJECT AND THE QUESTION IS "WHAT WILL THOU SAY WHEN HE SHALL PUNISH THEE?"

It is customary before sentence is passed for the guilty and condemned to say anything he wishes that might "favor him" or "touch the heart" of the judge. Place yourself before the blazing throne of God's judgment. What will you say?

A. Will you say it is unrighteous?
  1. God cannot be unrighteous.
  2. All the host of heaven will exclaim, "Righteous and holy art thou, O Lord God Almighty."
  3. Injustice with God is impossible. No just plea here.

B. Will you say it is too severe?
  1. That it exceeds your desert. That it would be cruel. God is never cruel. He is just the opposite.
  2. But since you have said no to the bleeding Son of God and shook your fist in the face of God, how can you say it is too severe?

C. Will you say you were not warned?
  1. Friends have warned you.
  2. Ministers have warned you.
  3. The Word of God warned you.
  4. Your conscience warned you.
  5. The Spirit of God warned you.

All these will testify against you. The mercy

and longsuffering of God will testify against you.

D. Will you plead for more time?
1. Like the servant that owed his master a debt, "Have patience with me. . . ." Matt. 18:26-29.
2. But, "The harvest is past, the summer is ended, and we are not saved." Jer. 8:20.
3. "He which is filthy, let him be filthy still." Rev. 22:11.

E. Will you confess your guilt and seek mercy?
1. This is good in time, but useless in eternity.
2. There is no throne of grace. There is no mercy, no spirit to strive, no promises, no gospel, no mediator, no hope!

F. Will you endeavor to resist the almighty arm?
1. There is no chance for the creature before the creator, none for finite before the infinite, weak before the strong, human against the divine.
2. He can, "destroy with the brightness of his coming." 2 Thess. 2:8.
3. "The mountains quake at him, and the hills melt, and the earth is burned at his presence. . . . Who can stand before his indignation? and who can abide in the fierceness of his anger? his fury is poured out like fire. . . ." Nahum 1:5, 6. ". . . who shall be able to stand?" Rev. 6:17.

G. Will you try to meet it with firmness?
1. Fear will come upon you like a desolation and destruction as a whirlwind. Prov. 1:27.
2. The stoutest hearts will quake and tremble. Your knees will smite one against the other, like Belshazzar. Dan. 5:5, 6.

3. "For our God is a consuming fire." Heb. 12:29.

CONCLUSION: Future punishment can be averted. You can escape the judgment. But not by neglecting and going on in sin. Heb. 2:3. But by REPENTANCE, Acts 3:19: "Repent . . . and be converted." By FORSAKING SIN, Isa. 55:7. By RESTITUTION, Luke 15:17-21. BELIEVING AND ACCEPTING Jesus Christ as Saviour and Lord, Acts 16:30-34.

Magnifying Christ

Phil. 1:20

INTRODUCTION: To magnify is to praise highly—to cause to be held in high esteem—to enlarge in fact or appearance—make objects appear larger than they are. Example: the magnifying glass.

Why does Christ need to be magnified? Isn't He big enough?

I. BECAUSE OF THE DISTANCE THE WORLD IS FROM HIM.

A. The Bible speaks about sinners being "far off." Eph. 2:13.

B. Some are close to church, but not to Him.

C. The world has isolated and insulated itself from Christ and the true biblical way of salvation. It is difficult to get them to see Him.

II. BECAUSE OF THE EXALTED OPINION OF THE WORLD.

A. The world thinks it is good enough.

B. With all its glamour, glitter, tinsel and artificial facade, it is satisfied. It will not humble itself before Him.

C. He must be exalted for them to consider Him.

D. If we just take our religion and Christ for granted, we will not effect them. We must be enthusiastic worshipers and workers.

III. BECAUSE THE DEVIL MAGNIFIES THE PLEASURES OF THE WORLD.

A. He makes pleasures look beautiful. He makes them look better than they are.

B. The Bible speaks about the *pleasure of sin, but only for a season.* Heb. 11:25.

C. "In thy presence is fulness of joy; at thy right hand there are pleasures for evermore." Psa. 16:11. This is true pleasure. Pleasures, not for a season, but pleasures forevermore.

D. It is "joy unspeakable and full of glory." 1 Pet. 1:8.

IV. BECAUSE OF THE LITTLENESS OF RELIGIOUS PROFESSORS.

Paul said, "Many walk . . . I have told you . . . weeping that they are the enemies of the cross of Christ." Phil. 3:18. So many profess and don't possess. The world cannot see Him in most who profess to know Him.

The testimony of a traveling salesman. He asked, "What is a Christian?" When he was told, he stated, "If what you say is so, then I have never seen a Christian."

A. Magnify Him by living a holy life.
We are the "light of the world." Matt. 5:14.
If we say we abide in him, we ought to "walk, even as he walked." 1 John 2:6.
"Be ye holy; for I am holy." 1 Pet. 1:16. This is God's standard . . . and it is what the unsaved expect of us.

B. Magnify Him by trusting Him.
Not by doubting and being fearful or by whining or complaining, but by trusting Jesus Christ. No one has ever magnified Christ by magnifying their troubles. Let people know we believe He is able. Eph. 3:20.

C. Magnify Him by separating from things that are questionable. When we yield to temptation we belittle the power of Christ. We are to shun even the appearance of evil. We are to come out from the world and be a separate people. 2 Cor. 6:17.

34

D. Magnify Him by praising Him.
"Let every thing that hath breath praise the Lord." Psa. 150:6.
David said he would praise Him "all the day long." Psa. 35:28.

E. Magnify Him by manifesting the Spirit He had. He was holy, harmless, undefiled. When He was reviled, He reviled not again. 1 Pet. 2:23. "If any man have not the Spirit of Christ, he. . . ." Rom. 8:9.
   1. *Results:* Our lives will then effect others and cause them to turn to Christ.
   2. It will make people want Him.
   3. It will cause the church to be built up.
   4. It will encourage other saints.

CONCLUSION: The appalling tragedy is that in some churches where Christ was once the center of attraction, now He stands outside knocking to get in again. Rev. 3:20. Their candlestick has been removed. Rev. 2:5. There is no power, nor presence of Christ. There is no spiritual warmth nor true worship. It (the church) is only going through a form of worship unnoticed and un-recognized by the great God of eternity. Let us be doubly sure that we magnify Him by life or death.

What Think Ye of Christ?

Matt. 22:42

INTRODUCTION: He was called wonderful, counsellor, mighty God, everlasting Father, Prince of Peace, the lily of the valley, the bright and morning star, the rock, the Word, Son of man, Son of God, Emmanuel, etc. Numbers of great men have said many complimentary things about Him; Livingstone, David Brainerd, Washington, Lincoln and others. But the New Testament contains many statements about Him, from those that had a confrontation with Him.

I. PILATE, AFTER EXAMING HIM.

   A. I find no fault in Him. Luke 23:14.

   B. He knew that the Jews, through envy, had delivered Jesus into his hands. Mark 15:10.

   C. Pilate could not wash this cowardly act off his hands or his conscience. Matt. 27:24.

II. PILATE'S WIFE, AFTER DREAMING ABOUT JESUS.

   A. She called Jesus a "just man."

   B. She told Pilate, "I have suffered many things . . . in a dream because of" this man. Matt. 27:19.

   C. He (Jesus) will bother your sleep or bless your sleep.

III. JUDAS, WHO BETRAYED HIM.

   A. "I have betrayed . . . innocent blood." Matt. 27:4.

   B. Man cannot buy or sell the Saviour. He must either accept Him or reject Him.

36

C. Judas realized the real truth and worth of Jesus too late.

IV. THE CENTURION, AFTER SEEING HIM DIE.

A. "Certainly this was a righteous man." Luke 23: 47. And again, "Truly this was the Son of God." Matt. 27:54.

B. It was said, "No man ever spake like this man," the centurion could say, "No man ever died like this man."

V. THE DEMONS WHO MET HIM.

A. "Jesus, thou Son of the most high God." Mark 5:7. And "Jesus, thou Son of God most high." Luke 8:28.

B. The demons in the demoniac recognized His divinity, even though some theologians do not.

VI. THE ANGELS.

A. "And thou shalt call his name Jesus: for. . . ." Matt. 1:21.

B. "For unto you is born this day in the city of David a Saviour, which is Christ the Lord." Luke 2:11.

C. "He shall be great, and shall be called the Son of the Highest." Luke 1:32.

D. This was a heavenly witness of His Sonship and His divinity.

VII. THE BLIND MEN.

A. They called him, "Thou son of David." Matt. 9:27-20:30.

B. They saw more than some others see who have 20-20 vision.

VIII. PAUL, THE APOSTLE TO THE GENTILES.

A. When the chief sinner met the Chief Shepherd (Jesus) on the Damascus Road, he cried out, "Who art thou, Lord?" He knew who He was because he called Him Lord. It is impossible to have a confrontation with Jesus Christ and not know who He is.

B. He soon responded to Jesus and said, "Lord, what wilt thou have me do?" Acts 9:4-6.

C. Paul called Jesus, "The blessed and only Potentate, the King of kings, and Lord of lords." 1 Tim. 6:15.

IX. ANDREW AFTER MEETING JESUS.

A. "We have found the Messias, which is, being interpreted, the Christ." John 1:41.

B. He believed Him to be the One the prophets had prophesied would come, the Messiah, the Redeemer.

X. JOHN THE BAPTIST.

A. The forerunner of Christ said, "Behold the Lamb of God. . . ." John 1:29.

B. And he said, "This is the Son of God." John 1:34.

C. Again he stated, "He [Jesus] must increase, but I must decrease." John 3:30.

XI. JOHN, THE BELOVED APOSTLE.

A. He declared, "He that hath the Son hath life. . . ." 1 John 5:12.

B. Again, "Jesus Christ, who is the faithful witness, and the first begotten of the dead, and the prince of the kings of the earth." Rev. 1:5.

C. Again he said Jesus would be "called Faithful

and True. . . . The Word of God. . . . Almighty
God. . . . King of kings, and Lord of lords."
Rev. 19:11-16.

XII. SIMON PETER.

A. "Thou art the Christ, the Son of the living
God." Matt. 16:16.

B. "And when the *chief Shepherd* shall appear.
. . ." 1 Peter 5:4.

XIII. PHILIP TESTIFYING TO NATHANAEL.

A. "We have found him, of whom Moses in the
law, and the prophets, did write, Jesus of
Nazareth, the son of Joseph." John 1:45.

B. He made the great discovery that Jesus was the
Messiah that was to come.

C. As a result, Nathanael declared, "Rabbi, thou
art the Son of God; thou . . . King of Israel."
John 1:49.

D. He recognized Jesus as God's Son, the redeemer
and future king and ruler of Israel.

XIV. THOMAS AFTER DOUBTING.

A. He acknowledged Him to be, "My Lord and
my God." John 20:28.

B. Thomas has been severely criticized for his
doubting. But even if this is justified, there are
two things that ought to be considered here.
First, he wanted to be sure ("Except I shall see
in his hands the print of the nails . . . I will not
believe"). Second, when he saw Jesus he
was thoroughly convinced that He had risen
from the dead. No other proof was necessary,
when he saw Jesus, he knew Him.

C. Jesus' statement to Thomas should be encouragement to every Christian, "Thomas, because

thou hast seen me, thou hast believed: blessed are they that have not seen, and yet have believed." V. 29.

CONCLUSION: What think ye of Christ? Do you believe He is the only begotten Son of God? Do you believe He is the only Saviour of men; the only potentate; the King of kings and Lord of lords; the Chief Shepherd, that is soon coming to gather His own unto that great heavenly sheepfold?

Consecration

1 Chron. 29:5

INTRODUCTION: It is said that the word *consecrate* in different forms is found in the Bible forty-two times. In the sense to "separate" three times; "to set apart" seven times; to "devote" and "dedicate" one time each. But "to fill" or "being filled" twenty-nine times.

I. TO SEPARATE FROM THE UNCLEAN.

A. The law of the Nazarite clearly taught this. Num. 6:1-13. To touch the unclean was to bring instant defilement and mar his holy relationship. This is no new doctrine. Remember Adam, Abel, Enoch and Noah.

B. It was taught in the calling of Abraham, in the lives of Patriarchs, Judges, Prophets and the Apostles.

C. The church is "the called out ones" by the grace of God; saints or separated ones. "Ye are not of the world, but I have chosen you *out of the world*. . . ." John 15:19.

"Wherefore come out from among them, and *be ye separate,* saith the Lord, and touch not the unclean thing; and. . . ." 2 Cor. 6:17.

D. So consecration is to separate yourself from all uncleanness. Uncleanness of Spirit as well as body. 2 Cor. 7:1: ". . . let us cleanse ourselves from all filthiness of the flesh and spirit. . . ."

II. TO BE SET APART FOR GOD.

A. Separation does not mean isolation. Psa. 4:3: "The Lord hath *set apart* him that is godly for himself."

B. By the holy anointing, Aaron and his sons, were

41

set apart (consecrated) that, they might minister unto the Lord. Ex. 30:30.

C. The vessels of the tabernacle were "set apart" for God's service by being anointed.

D. The vessels, though new, were unfit for service until they received the baptism of holy oil. They were sanctified and meet for use as soon as they occupied their true place and were set apart by anointing oil.

E. Who will set himself apart for service? It is the same to us. 1 Thess. 4:3, 4: "This is the will of God, even your sanctification, that . . . possess his vessel in sanctification and honour." 2 Tim. 2:21: "If a man therefore purge himself from these, he shall be a vessel unto honour, sanctified, and meet for the master's use, and prepared unto every good work."

III. TO BE DEVOTED TO GOD.

A. It was said of Jericho, "the city shall be devoted and all that is therein to the Lord." Jos. 6:17 (Revised Version). Achan took the devoted thing and brought trouble on the camp and condemnation on himself.

B. It is a warning to us, never to take anything for our own selfish use, that is devoted to God. "Ye are not your own . . . ye are bought with a price." 1 Cor. 6:19, 20.

C. 1 Sam. 1:11: Samuel was devoted to God "all the days of his life." Every offering laid upon the altar was devoted to God. *It would have been sin to take it back.*

D. The servant with a bored ear became forever devoted to his master. Ex. 21:7.

E. Who is willing to devote himself unto the Lord? Rom. 12:1: "I beseech you therefore, brethren

42

. . . that ye present your bodies a living sacrifice.
. . ." The disciples, *First gave themselves to the Lord,* then their time, talents and money—their all. 2 Chron. 31:6: "They also brought in the tithe of oxen and sheep, and the tithe of holy things which were consecrated unto the Lord their God, and laid them by *heaps."*

IV. TO HAVE HANDS FILLED FOR THE SERVICE OF GOD.

A. The word *consecrate* was used twenty-nine times in the sense of "filling the hands." So, the most prominent thought in connection with consecration is not giving, but taking, not yielding, but receiving.

B. The marginal reading of the text is "who then offereth *willingly* to *fill* his hands this day unto the Lord." God does not want us to serve with empty hands.

C. Jesus did not send away the hungry multitude, because the disciples did not have enough to satisfy them. He filled their hands with heaven-sent bread and so equipped them to carry out His will.

D. Are our hands so filled with Christ, the "Bread of God," the "Bread of Life" that hungry souls are being satisfied?

E. Empty hands are powerless hands. We cannot bless people with empty hands. Our hands are full of too many other things. They should be filled with God's sufficiency.

CONCLUSION: Our hands will hang down in feebleness and emptiness, until they are given to the Lord. The priest's hands were filled only after they were cleansed and anointed. So must we be cleansed and anointed before our hands are filled for service unto God.

The Effects of Pentecost

Acts 2:1-4

INTRODUCTION: When a man is baptized with the Holy Ghost, a great change takes place. There is *DEEPER HUMILITY,* because of a deeper sense of unworthiness. And *A MORE HOLY SOBRIETY,* because of a keener consciousness of how easily the Spirit may be grieved. *THIS MIGHTY AND PRECIOUS ANOINTING,* is not put upon man's flesh (old self-seeking nature) that it might minister to his pride. "No flesh should glory in his presence." 1 Cor. 1:29.

The Spirit was not given until Christ was glorified and until we are prepared to glorify Him at any cost, we need not expect a baptism of the Spirit. This is the reason so many people are without this blessing. Christ is not exalted to the throne of their hearts. In this message, let us talk about some of the prominent results that follow this spiritual baptism.

I. GREAT AMAZEMENT. Acts 2:7-12.

    A. "They were all amazed. . . ." In other words they were confounded, marveled, were in doubt, mocked, etc. Here is something they could not deny, yet couldn't understand.

    B. The natural man cannot understand spiritual things. 1 Cor. 2:14: "But the natural man *receiveth not* the things of the Spirit of God: for they are foolishness unto him: *neither can he know them,* because. . . ."

    C. 1 Cor. 2:4, 5: "And my speech and my preaching *was* not with enticing words of man's wisdom, but in demonstration of the Spirit and of power: *That* your faith should not stand in the wisdom of men, but in the power of God."

    D. The Holy Ghost baptized man's speech and

44

preaching is powerful. If the Spirit is present
HE WILL DEMONSTRATE HIS OWN
PRESENCE.

II. GOD WILL BE GLORIFIED.

A. "We do hear them speak in our tongues the wonderful works of God." V. 11.

B. "If ye be reproached for the name of Christ,
happy are ye; for the spirit of glory and of God
resteth upon you: on their part he is evil spoken
of, but on your part he is glorified." 1 Pet. 4:14.

C. When you are filled with the Spirit, the world is
sure to assail you, but the Spirit of God resteth
upon you.

D. Count it joy for God will be glorified. James
1:2. When self was exalted God was dishonored,
now self is fallen like Dagon and God is
enthroned.

III. CONTINUAL FELLOWSHIP

A. "And they continued stedfastly in the apostles'
doctrine and fellowship. . . ." Acts 2:42.

B. "But the anointing which ye have received of
him abideth in you, and ye need not that any
man teach you. . . ." 1 John 2:27.

C. In John 14:16, Jesus said, "that he may abide
with you for ever." Our fellowship will be con-
tinuous, unless pride and unbelief mars our communion.

D. Speaks of "fellowship of the Spirit." It means
to have things in common. Is there such a day
in your experience? Is fellowship yet real? Fellowship in prayer—in service, etc.

E. Samuel anointed David and the Spirit of the Lord
came upon him "from that day forward." 1 Sam.
16:13.

IV. HOLY BOLDNESS

A. When they saw the boldness of Peter and John they took knowledge of them that they had been with Jesus. Acts 4:13. This implies Jesus was bold.

B. Gideon was bold when he threw down the altar of Baal. The Spirit of the Lord came upon him and he blew a trumpet. Judges 6:34.

C. When men are Spirit-filled and fire-baptized they cannot help but blow the trumpet in Zion.

D. Peter and John were filled with the Spirit and said, "we cannot but speak the things which we have seen and heard." Acts 4:20.

E. Men may get tired hearing it, but we cannot hold our peace. They frown on us and persecute us, belittle us and bemean us but we must continue for Jesus' sake. We must continue to testify of the Pentecostal power. We denounce sin, we preach that men must repent and we preach there is a judgment to come.

V. POWERFUL TESTIMONY

A. They were all filled with the Holy Ghost and with great power gave the apostles witness of the resurrection of the Lord Jesus. Acts 4:31-33.

B. "His word was with power." Luke 4:32.

C. Stephen was full of the Holy Ghost and they (the people) were not able to resist the Spirit by which he spake. Acts 6:10. The men disputed with Stephen, but they were no match for his powerful, Spirit-filled preaching.

D. "Not by might, nor by power, but. . . ." Zech. 4:6. "I am full of power by the spirit of the Lord." Micah 3:8. He goes on to say, "to de-

46

clare unto Jacob his transgression, and to Israel his sin."

E. We need this power today to declare the whole counsel of God, keeping back nothing. Paul said, ". . . I kept back nothing that was profitable unto you. . . ." Acts 20:20. "I have not shunned to declare unto you all the counsel of God." V. 27. Our power for God will be in proportion as we work with the Spirit of God.

VI. MIGHTY WORKS

A. The Spirit of the Lord came upon Samson, and he rent a lion as he would rent a kid. Judges 14:6. Also, other mighty works: Acts 5:12-16; Acts 3:1-8; 5:1-11.

B. Spirit-filled men handle lions as if they were kids.

C. "Greater works. . . ." John 14:12.

D. Devils cast out, healings, prisons unlocked, etc.

VII. FRAGRANT INFLUENCE

A. "They took knowledge of them, that they had been with Jesus." Acts 4:13.

B. "God, thy God, hath anointed thee with the oil of gladness above thy fellows. All thy garments smell of myrrh, and aloes, and cassia, out of the ivory palaces, whereby they have made thee glad." Psa. 45:7, 8.

C. These garments of fragrance cover the anointed ones. This influence is not put on for special occasions. This fragrance was on *ALL THY GARMENTS!*

D. It is on our work clothes as well as our church clothes. *"Garment of praise."* Isa. 61:3.

CONCLUSION: Full of the Holy Ghost, filled so full there is no room for anything else. Pentecostal works will follow.

What Brings You to Calvary?

John 19:25

INTRODUCTION: Many people came to Calvary on that day. Some came with groups, others as individuals. All of them had a reason or purpose for being at the scene of this inhuman, unreasonable and illegal crucifixion of Jesus.

I. ECCLESIASTICAL LEADERS

A. They came to see the suffering of the person who had challenged their leadership. He had unsparingly rebuked them in His preaching.

B. These chief priests, rulers, scribes, elders and Jews wanted, even demanded, Christ to be crucified (John 19:6, 7), and they persuaded the multitude to ask for Barabbas instead of Christ. They made their choice between good and evil. Matt. 27:20; Mark 15:11.

C. Even though Pilate and Herod had found no fault in Jesus, they still wanted Him killed and Barabbas released. Luke 23:10-15.

D. They were there to coerce and threaten Pilate and force him to bow to their demands. They hated Jesus and wanted Him crucified.

II. THE SOLDIERS

A. They came because of duty. It was their job.

B. They stripped Him and put on Him the scarlet robe.

C. They crowned Him with thorns, mocked Him, spit on Him, smote Him, cast lots for His robe, and pierced His side. Matt. 27:27-31.

D. Every man is either a soldier (a Christian, a

48

friend) of the cross or a soldier (a sinner, an enemy) at the cross.

III. PILATE CAME BECAUSE IT WAS HIS OFFICIAL DUTY

A. He took no delight doing his duty on this day. He knew Jesus was delivered unto him because of envy. Matt. 27:18.

B. And he knew Jesus was guilty of no crime. Matt. 27:23.

C. He acceded to the demands of the people. Mark 15:15. Because of fear and weakness he delivered up to death the guiltless and set free the guilty. This happens in every generation; this yielding to pressure of people and compromising right and worthy principles because of fear of losing favor, prestige, power and position.

D. Examples: The politician, church leaders, clergymen, businessmen, educators, and contemporary society.

E. He took water, washed his hands and declared, "I am innocent of the blood of this just person." Matt. 27:24. But this did not make him innocent. He should have stood for the evidence (or lack of it), and for what he believed in his heart about Jesus.

IV. THE MULTITUDE

A. *Some came because of anger and hatred.* These included the lawyers, Pharisees, hypocrites, etc. He had challenged, charged, rebuked and completely disrobed them. Matt. 6:5, 16; Matt. 23: 13, 15, 46, 48.

B. *Some came out of curiosity.* This always happens at momentous occasions. It has happened in this country at public lynchings. They were

49

perhaps (1) anxious to see how it would be done, (2) to know how they would feel and react to a violent death, and (3) perhaps to see who would be there.

C. *Others came out of sympathy.* Some were not followers of Jesus, but believed Him to be a good man. They knew He had helped and healed many people, so they came out of respect and sympathy.

They sympathized with what they believed to be His unfortunate and untimely death. "And there followed him a great company of people, and of women, which also bewailed and lamented him." Luke 23:27.

V. THE DISCIPLES CAME BECAUSE OF LOYALTY

A. John, the beloved disciple, was there. John 19:25.

B. "Joseph of Arimathaea, being a disciple of Jesus, but secretly for fear of the Jews," came for the body of Jesus. John 19:38.

C. Nicodemus was there with a mixture of myrrh and aloes, to help in the burial. John 19:39, 40.

D. Some, regretfully, had forsaken Him and fled out of fear and one had denied he knew Him. Mark 14:50.

E. We must never stop short of Calvary! VV. 66-72.

VI. THE TWO THIEVES

A. In their case it was unavoidable. They were there against their will. They were unwilling observers and participators at this dreadful event. Mark 15:7, John 18:40, Luke 23:25.

B. They were guilty of crime. No question was

50

raised by them or others about their guilt. It was a well proven fact.

C. The guiltless, spotless and undefiled Lamb of God died between these guilty criminals. It was a reproachful death. Heb. 13:12, 13. One thief accepted Jesus. The other rejected Him. One went into paradise with Jesus, the other to the eternal abode of the wicked.

VII. WHAT CAN BE FOUND AT CALVARY?

A. *Forgiveness.* While hanging on the cross, *Jesus prayed, "Father, forgive them;* for they know not what they do." Luke 23:34.

B. *Cleansing.* Zech. 13:1, tells us that "In that day there shall be a fountain opened . . . for sin and for uncleanness." The soldiers ". . . pierced his side, and forthwith came there out blood and water." John 19:34. ". . . the blood of Jesus Christ his Son cleanseth us from all sin." 1 John 1:7. ". . . cleanse us from all unrighteousness." V. 9.

C. *Healing.* ". . . with his stripes we are healed." Isa. 53:5. ". . . by whose stripes ye were healed." 1 Peter 2:24. ". . . Himself took our infirmities, and bare our sicknesses." Matt. 8:17. ". . . I am the Lord that healeth thee." Ex. 15:26.

CONCLUSION: Christians come to Calvary first, because of loyalty to Him. Second, because He is our only hope. There is no other way. John 14:6, Acts 4:12. And third, because He will meet our need, both in time and in eternity.

They Know Not What They Do

Luke 23:34

INTRODUCTION: Most times when this text is used, only the part "Father forgive them" is fully discussed. The latter part is important also for it shows how unaware the crucifiers were of the magnitude of this murder. They were totally ignorant of what they were doing.

I. THEY KNEW NOT THAT THEY WERE FUL-FILLING PROPHECY.

   A. They should have known, but they did not. Their sin was inexcusable.

   B. Psalm 22 foretells this terrible event.
      "My God, my God, why hast thou forsaken me?" V. 1.
      "He trusted on the Lord that he would deliver him: let him deliver him, seeing he delighted in him. V. 8.
      "They part my garments among them, and cast lots upon my vesture." V. 18.

   C. Psalm 69:21 states, ". . . in my thirst they gave me vinegar to drink."

   D. In Psalm 2:2, "The kings of the earth set themselves, and the rulers take counsel together, against the Lord, and against his anointed."

   E. Isaiah 50:6: "I gave my back to the smiters, and my cheeks to them that plucked off the hair: I hid not my face from shame and spitting."

   F. Isaiah 63:3: "I have trodden the winepress alone; and of the people there was none with me."

   G. Psalm 34:20: "He keepeth all his bones: not one of them is broken."

H. Isaiah 53:3-8, 12, gives a detailed account of the suffering, trial and crucifixion.

I. And Zech. 12:10 declared, ". . . they shall look upon me whom they have pierced."

II. THEY KNEW NOT THAT THEY WERE CRUCIFYING THE LORD OF GLORY.

A. The Apostle Paul said, ". . . had they known it, they would not have crucified the Lord of glory." 1 Cor. 2:8.

B. In his Pentecost Day sermon, Peter declared, "Therefore let all the house of Israel know assuredly, that God hath made that same Jesus, whom ye have crucified, both Lord and Christ." Acts 2:36.

C. Acts 5:30, 31: "The God of our fathers raised up Jesus, whom ye slew and hanged on a tree. . . . God exalted with his right hand to be a Prince and a Saviour."

D. 1 Cor. 15:47: ". . . the second man [Jesus Christ] is the Lord from heaven."

E. When He comes again, it will be final proof He ·is the·Lord of Glory, "The Lord himself shall descend from heaven. . . ." 1 Thess. 4:16-18.

III. THEY KNEW NOT THAT THEY WERE REJECTING GOD'S GIFT TO MAN.

A. "For God so loved the world, that he gave his only begotten Son. . . ." John 3:16.
"For God sent not his Son into the world to condemn the world; but that the world through him might be saved." V. 17.

B. Rom. 6:23: ". . . but the gift of God is eternal life. . . ."

C. 2 Cor. 9:15: "Thanks be unto God for his unspeakable gift."

D. Matt. 21:42: ". . . The stone which the builders rejected, the same is become the head of the corner. . . ."

E. 1 Peter 2:7: ". . . the stone which the builders disallowed, the same is. . . ."

F. They crucified their only hope. Acts 4:12.

IV. THEY KNEW NOT THAT THEY WERE BEING USED OF SATAN.

A. ". . . the devil having now put into the heart of Judas Iscariot, Simon's son, to betray him. . . ." John 13:2.

"And after the sop Satan entered into him [Judas]." V. 27.

B. The devil used Judas to betray Jesus "into the hands of sinners." Matt. 26:45; Mark 14:41.

C. Stephen preached to a crowd that stoned him to death. One thing he said was that your fathers persecuted the prophets and slew the ones which showed the coming of the *Just One* (Jesus) "of whom ye have been now the betrayers and murderers. . . ." Acts 7:52.

D. ". . . ye slew and hanged [Him] on a tree." Acts 5:30; 10:39.

E. *Matthew Henry* states, "The devil put it in the heart of Judas to betray Christ, of Peter to deny Him, of the Chief Priests to prosecute Him, and Pilate to condemn Him."

V. THEY KNEW NOT THEY COULD ONLY DO THIS BECAUSE GOD ALLOWED IT TO FULFILL HIS DIVINE PLAN.

A. "Yet it pleased the Lord to bruise him; he hath put him to grief: *when thou shalt make his soul an offering for sin. . . .*" Isaiah 53:10.

B. "Him [Jesus], being *delivered by the determinate counsel and foreknowledge of God,* ye have taken, and by wicked hands have crucified and slain." Acts 2:23; Luke 22:22.

C. Jesus told Pilate, "Thou couldest have no power at all against me, *except it were given thee from above. . . ."* John 19:11.

VI. THEY KNEW NOT THAT THIS WAS IN REALITY A DEFEAT FOR SATAN.

A. "And I will put enmity between thee and the woman, and between thy seed and her seed; it shall bruise thy head, and thou shalt bruise his heel." Gen. 3:15.

B. Heb. 2:14: ". . . that through death he *might destroy him that had the power of death, that is, the devil."*

C. ". . . the Son of God was manifested, that he might destroy the works of the devil." 1 John 3:8.

D. "And having spoiled principalities and powers, he made a shew of them openly, triumphing over them in it." Col. 2:15. *Phillips Translation* states, "He exposed them, shattered, empty and defcated, in his final glorious triumphant act."

VII. THEY KNEW NOT THAT JESUS WAS TO BE THE FUTURE WORLD RULER.

A. John 19:19: "Pilate wrote a title, and put it on the cross. . . . *Jesus of Nazareth the King of the Jews."* The Jews rejected it and complained to Pilate. V. 21.

B. There will be a day when He will not only be King of the Jews, but King (ruler) of the whole world. Isaiah prophesied, ". . . Of the increase of his government and peace there shall be no end. . . ." Isaiah 9:6, 7.

C. Rev. 17:14: ". . . and the Lamb shall overcome them: for he is *Lord* of lords, and *King* of kings. . . ."

D. After the great tribulation when heaven is opened and Christ returns to earth on a white horse, He will have on His vesture and on His thigh a name written *KING OF KINGS, AND LORD OF LORDS.* Rev. 19:11-16.

CONCLUSION: The biblical description of this scene is too great for mortal tongue to fully describe. Men should search the Scriptures, ". . . for in them ye think ye have eternal life. . . ." John 5:39. Many "err, not knowing the scriptures, nor the power of God." Matt. 22:29. Men "err in their heart. . . ." Heb. 3:10. The only assurance against spiritual ignorance is to know Jesus Christ. 1 John 2:3; 3:24; 4:13.

The Solemn Caution

Heb. 3:7-11

INTRODUCTION: *The History of the Jews* is full of instructions and warnings. It shows the deep depravity of the heart for they continually murmured and sinned against God. "The heart is deceitful above all things, and desperately wicked. . . ." Jer. 17:9. God was making the heaven and the earth to serve them with manna, water and quails. The *History of the Jews* shows how slow God is to anger, how extensive in mercy; how patient and longsuffering toward these erring people. But sinful and impenitent people will not finally be allowed to escape. If His grace is despised, and His mercy rejected, He will not spare the guilty.

Let us consider *His Voice:*

I. IT IS THE VOICE OF MERCY.

   A. Grace poured forth from His lips. He came not to condemn, John 3:17: "For God sent not his Son into the world to. . . ." Not to curse, but to bless.

   B. "The Spirit of the Lord is upon me. . . ." Luke 4:18, 19.

   C. He had compassion. He opened wide His heart and arms. Matt. 11:28-30.

   D. "All manner of sin and blasphemy shall be forgiven . . . but. . . ." Matt. 12:31. "I am come that they might have life, and that they might have it more abundantly." John 10:10. "For he taught them as *one* having authority, and not as the scribes. Matt. 7:29. No man spake like Him.

II. IT WAS THE VOICE OF DIVINE AUTHORITY.
   He was the sent, the anointed, the divine authority,

57

the law. To despise Moses meant death, Heb. 10: 28, 29, "He that despised . . . how much sorer punishment . . . trodden under foot the Son of God. . . ."

III. HIS IS THE ONLY VOICE THAT CAN GIVE SALVATION.

None can give rest to weary, but Christ.
None can invite to supper, but Christ.
None can speak away guilt, but Christ.
None can give peace to distracted souls, but Christ.
None can pronounce the reward of everlasting life, but Christ.
None other Name under heaven. . . . Acts 4:12.

IV. THE VOICE ADDRESSES US THROUGH VARIOUS MEANS OF COMMUNICATION.

A. The written word, " . . . the words that I speak unto you, they are spirit, and they are life." John 6:63. They are the words of Christ. Rom. 1:16; Heb. 4:12.

B. By the Spirit. Gen. 6:3; Heb. 3:7, 8.

C. Events of providence (Alarm clock method) trouble—wrecks—death, etc. *All these under control of Christ.*

V. THERE IS A SPECIFIED PERIOD FOR HEARING HIS VOICE.

"To day if ye will hear his voice, Harden not your hearts. . . ." Heb. 3:7, 8. The gospel dispensation is represented as a day, a limited period.

A. *It is short, only a day.*
How soon it will terminate. There is much to be done in so short a time. Job 14:1, 2. Only one life will soon be past. Time is running out.

B. *It is uncertain as well as short.*
1. "Boast not thyself of to morrow." Prov. 27:1.

58

2. What is your life? James 4:14.

3. ". . . sun is gone down while it was yet day.
   . . ." Jer. 15:9.

4. Succeeded by the darkness and stillness of the
   grave!

5. No device or work there. No voice of mercy.
   No preaching, no promise. So it is necessary
   to hear, ". . . man goeth to his long home,
   and the mourners go about the streets." Ecc.
   12:5.

VI. THERE IS YET ANOTHER CAUTION.

A. "Harden not your heart. . . ." We harden our
   hearts by inattention to the concern of our soul.
   The natural tendency is to hardness, we must
   yield to the influences of the Word, Spirit, etc.

B. *Beginning of wisdom"* is to fear God. Prov. 9:10.

C. God said to Moses concerning Israel, *"Oh! That
   they were wise."*

D. "He, that being often reproved hardeneth his
   neck, shall. . . ." Prov. 29:1.

E. *We harden our hearts by pursuing the works of
   darkness.* These all harden men's hearts, steel
   the mind, blunt the feelings and pervert the
   faculties of the soul.

F. *We harden our hearts by yielding to the influences of unbelief.*

   1. Unbelief—darkens the mind and petrifies the
      heart. It resists all evidence and stays the
      wonder-working power of Christ.

   2. For He could not do many mighty works there
      because of their unbelief. Matt. 13:58.

   3. They entered not because of unbelief. Heb.
      3:19.

59

G. *We harden our hearts by attaching ourselves to this present world.*

1. The love of the world leads the heart to hardness.

2. The love of the world concentrates all its power on this present world and loses sight of heaven and God's crown of glory. 1 John 2: 15-17.

CONCLUSION: You are responsible, for the voice of Christ has repeatedly sounded in your ears. If you hear, harden not your heart. No one can answer for you. You have your day, but when it is over, it is too late. How necessary then that you hear, believe, accept, and begin life anew. Do it today for tomorrow may never come. Prov. 1:24-28.

Walking With God

Gen. 5:22-24

INTRODUCTION: Enoch's epitaph is only one sentence, but it is an impressive one; "Enoch walked with God." It is said of Noah that "he moved with fear and prepared an ark to the saving of his house." And of Moses that "The law came by Moses." It is said of David that "he served his generation and fell on sleep." Paul was "a bondservant of Jesus Christ." History records that after Alexander "conquered the world he sat down and wept because there was no more worlds to conquer." And it was said of George Washington, that he was "first in war, first in peace and first in the hearts of his countrymen." But "Enoch walked with God." *What an experience!* WALKING WITH GOD!

We read of walking before, after and with God. Walking before God is the walk of perfection. Gen. 17:1. Walking after God is the walk of obedience. Deut. 13:4. Walking with God is the walk of friendship and fellowship. Gen. 5:24.

Walking with God implies harmony, friendship and fellowship. 1 John 1:3, 7.

God desires that we walk with Him. Matthew Henry says, "Walking with God pleases Him." *"There are at least three reasons why Enoch walked with God."*

I. ENOCH WAS CAREFUL ABOUT HIS COMPANIONS.

    A. You cannot walk with God and walk with those out of harmony with Him. One cannot walk with the riffraff of this world and with the righteous, Holy, Almighty God at the same time. Enoch would not walk "in the counsel of the ungodly." Psa. 1:1.

    B. He knew that "evil communications corrupt good

61

manners." 1 Cor. 15:33. *Amplified:* ". . . Evil companionship (communion, associations) corrupt and deprave good manners and morals and character."

C. God said about Israel, they "walked . . . in the way of Jeroboam the son of Nebat, who made Israel to sin." 1 Kings 22:52.

D. We must be careful about our companions, for how "Can two walk together, except they be agreed?" Amos 3:3.

E. "Be ye not unequally yoked together with unbelievers. . . . what part hath he that believeth with an infidel?" 2 Cor. 6:14-16.

F. Enoch chose to walk with God. He chose the best companion available.

II. SECOND, ENOCH WAS CERTAIN ABOUT HIS CONSECRATION.

A. He walked and lived so close to God that he had this testimony, "that he pleased God." Heb. 11:5. In this same verse it says, "Enoch was translated that he should not see death . . . God . . . translated him."

B. "And Enoch walked with God: and he was not; for God took him." (Text)

C. He could say as David, ". . . I will walk in thy truth." Psa. 86:11.

D. And as Micah, ". . . we will walk in the name of the Lord our God for ever and ever." Micah 4:5.

E. Whatever the cost in sacrifice, submission or suffering, Enoch was determined to walk with God. To him this was the most pleasant and profitable profession he could possibly pursue.

62

III. THIRD, ENOCH WAS CAUTIOUS ABOUT HIS DIRECTIONS.

A. Direction determines destiny and direction is determined by decision.

B. Lot pitched his tent toward Sodom. Gen. 13:12. The results of that choice is well known.
   1. He lost his heart in Sodom.
   2. He lost his home.
   3. He lost his happiness.
   4. And most tragic, he lost his spirituality.

C. But Enoch walked with God. He went in God's direction. He kept in step with Him. He kept his eyes on God, not man.

D. God's ways are not like our ways. Isaiah 55:7, 8. We must forsake our way if we are to walk in harmony with Him. V. 7.

E. Walking with God implies . . .
   1. prestige—as to spiritual status
   2. privilege—as to sonship
   3. perfection—as to sainthood.

How are we to walk with God?
   1. "For we walk by faith, not by sight." 2 Cor. 5:7.
   2. ". . . we walk in the light. . . ." 1 John 1:7.
   3. Walk in the "newness of life." Rom. 6:4.
   4. Walk in the Spirit. Gal. 5:16.
   5. Walk circumspectly. Eph. 5:15, 16.
   6. Walk worthily. Eph. 4:1.
   7. Walk in love. Eph. 5:2.

CONCLUSION: "In all thy ways acknowledge him, and he shall direct thy paths." Prov. 3:6.

Days That Speak to Us

Job 32:7

INTRODUCTION: There are many great days recorded in the Word of God. They include the day of creation, the day of atonement, the day of Pentecost and the day of the Lord. We will concern ourselves with only three in this message: yesterday, today and tomorrow. These days speak very clearly to us and we should heed their advice.

I. YESTERDAY SPEAKS.

It says unto us, "I am gone, but learn of me." There is no way to go back to yesterday and straighten out mistakes and unsolved problems. Oh, how some of us would like to go back and change some things, but it utterly is impossible. The door is closed. Yesterday is in the unreachable past. It is gone forever!

A. Though yesterday cannot be relived, our *Lord would have us remember our mistakes and learn from them.* Some of us have faltered many times this past year. Let us learn from these mistakes and misunderstandings of yesterday. We can profit from them and avoid doing them again.

B. *Let us learn the futility of fighting our own battles.* It is said, "Experience is the best teacher." If so, we should have already learned that lesson and learned it well. Jesus tell us, ". . . without me ye can do nothing." John 15:5. But Paul declared, "I can do all things through Christ which strengtheneth me." Phil. 4:13. ". . . with God all things are possible." Matt. 19:26. Again the Word declares, ". . . greater is he that is in you, than he that is in the world." 1 John 4:4. His help is available at all times. We not only need His help, but we must have it if we are to be conquerors in this great battle.

64

C. *Let us learn that victorious Christian living is not possible without daily prayer and Bible reading.* When we pray, we talk to God. When we read His Word, He talks to us. Many Christians (especially young converts) fail at this point. The Psalmist declared, ". . . in his law doth he meditate day and night." Psalm 1:2. Job said, ". . . I have esteemed the words of his mouth more than my necessary food." Job 23:12. His Word is our strength and our guide.

D. *Let us remember that our happiest moments were when we were fully obeying God.* We should look back and reminisce over those blessed, happy days. Following afar off is a miserable life. Living "near to the heart of God" is the happy life. Let us recall the lukewarm, lackadaisical times when we walked away off from His presence and remember again that "happy is that people whose God is the Lord."

E. *Finally, let us remember that after we profit by mistakes and faults and are forgiven, it is best to forget them.* There is no value in mulling over and mourning about things that happened yesterday. Paul declared, ". . . this one thing I do, forgetting those things which are behind, and reaching forth unto those things which are before, *I press toward the mark for the prize* of the high calling of God in Christ Jesus." Phil. 3:13, 14.

II. TODAY SPEAKS.

It says, "I am at your service, use me." Yesterday is gone. There is no way to bring it back and no way to go back to it. It is foolish to grieve about past failures; or about what might have been. The story of Humpty Dumpty illustrates this point.

Humpty Dumpty sat on a wall;
Humpty Dumpty had a great fall.

All the king's horses and all the king's men
Couldn't put Humpty Dumpty back together again."

How true this is! You cannot change things that happened yesterday. Yesterday is finished! It is ended forever!

A. *Today is here . . . use it.*

Today is the day of salvation, now is the accepted time. Heb. 3:8. Now, today is the all-important day. God says *"Come now,* and let us reason together, saith the Lord."* Isaiah 1:18. Today speaks loud and clear, "I will soon be gone, use me while you can. For I will soon be another yesterday."

1. *Use me for prayer and Bible study.* This is so important it ought to be done today, and too, you cannot make up tomorrow that which is neglected and lost today. And most importantly, you need the strength and direction they provide for today.

2. *Use me for doing good deeds for others.* There are many opportunities today that could be lost by procrastination or laziness. There are lost men and women all around us. Sickness is everywhere, spiritual sickness, physical sickness and mental sickness. Let us have compassion and do something for them today.

3. *Use me for praising the Lord.* He is worthy, so praise Him today. There is so little praising of our Lord, we should make up for the spiritual anemics, the lukewarm and careless ones. We can do it by praising God more and more each day. The need is now. Let's do it today.

4. *Use me for personal soulwinning.* The fields are white unto harvest today, let us reap the golden grain ere it perish in the field. We

66

must work the work of the One who called us and sent us for "the night cometh, when no man can work." John 9:4. If we put things off until tomorrow they may never get done.

III. TOMORROW SPEAKS.

It says "Don't worry about me, trust me with God." Many people fret and fume about the future. They say it looks so dark and there seems to be no way out.

A. It is true that we live in a day of uncertainty, a day of frustration, wickedness and utter confusion. It is a day when "Men's hearts failing them for fear, and for looking after those things which are coming on the earth." Luke 21:25-28.

Paul states, "This know also, that in the last days perilous times shall come. For men shall be lovers of their own selves, covetous, boasters, proud, blasphemers, disobedient to parents, unthankful, unholy. . . ." 2 Timothy 3:1-5.

Paul declares again, "For the time will come when they will not endure sound doctrine; but after their own lusts shall they heap to themselves teachers, having itching ears; And they shall turn away their ears from the truth, and shall be turned unto fables." 2 Timothy 4:3, 4.

B. *But even though there is darkness, despair and even desperation in the earth, God still sits on His throne in the heavenly world.* He still lives! Rev. 1:18. There are battles to fight but the same God who helped us fight them yesterday and is helping us today, will be with us in all our conflicts tomorrow. For His Word declares, "Jesus Christ the same yesterday, and to day, and for ever." Heb. 13:8. And "If God be for us, who can be against us?" Rom. 8:31.

C. *And what about these powerful words,* "Nay, in all these things we are more than conquerors through him

67

that loved us. For I am persuaded, that neither death, nor life, nor angels, nor principalities, nor powers, nor things present, nor things to come, Nor height, nor depth, nor any other creature, shall be able to separate us from the love of God, which is in Christ Jesus our Lord." (Rom. 8:37-39).

D. *Finally, let us adhere to Paul's advice and forget things behind and reach forth for those things before us.*

CONCLUSION: We cannot remedy the past, but we can make straight our path today and do the work assigned unto us. And thank God we can trust tomorrow with our never-failing heavenly Father. And above all else let us remember our Lord has promised to return for us someday and take us to His heavenly home where there will be everlasting peace and joy. We know who holds tomorrow. Let us trust Him until the end of the way.

Three Indispensables

INTRODUCTION: We can get along better without some things. And even though some things are needful, we can dispense with them. But here are three things that are absolutely indispensable to us. We cannot get to heaven without them.

I. THE BLOOD OF JESUS IS INDISPENSABLE.

A. Heb. 9:22: "And almost all things are by the law purged with blood; *and without shedding of blood is no remission.*"

B. 1 Peter 1:18, 19: "Forasmuch as ye know that ye were not redeemed with corruptible things, as silver and gold. . . . But with the precious blood of Christ, as of a lamb without blemish and without spot."

C. Rom. 5:9: "Much more then, being now justified by his blood, we shall be saved from wrath through him."

D. Eph. 1:7: "In whom we have redemption through his blood, the forgiveness of sins. . . ."

Many professors and preachers are saying, away with the blood, but, it is indispensable. Without the efficacy of the shed blood of Jesus, Christianity has no cause to justify its continuance.

II. FAITH IS INDISPENSABLE.

A. Heb. 11:6: *"But without faith it is impossible to please him:* for he that cometh to God must believe that he is, and that he is a rewarder of them that diligently seek him."

B. Rom. 5:1: "Therefore being justified by faith, we have peace with God through our Lord Jesus Christ."

C. Mark 5:34: "Daughter, thy faith hath made thee whole; go in peace, and be whole of thy plague."

D. Let us have faith in the unlimited ability of God. Mark 11:24: "What things soever ye desire, when ye pray, believe that ye receive them, and ye shall have them."

III. HOLINESS IS INDISPENSABLE.

A. Heb. 12:14: "Follow peace with all men, *and holiness, without which no man shall see the Lord.*"

B. Lev. 11:44: "For I am the Lord your God: ye shall therefore sanctify yourselves, and ye shall be holy; for I am holy. . . ."

C. 1 Peter 1:16: "Because it is written, Be ye holy; for I am holy."

"Be ye holy; for I am holy," is found in both Old and New Testaments. Holiness is God's standard. God requires nothing higher and accepts nothing lower.

D. Titus 2:11, 12: "For the grace of God that bringeth salvation hath appeared to all men, Teaching us that, denying ungodliness and worldly lusts, we should live soberly, righteously, and godly, in this present world."

CONCLUSION: The blood of Jesus, faith and holiness are indispensables in the believer's salvation and his daily walk with God.

Woman, God's Incomparable Creature

(Mother's Day Sermon)

Proverbs 31:10

INTRODUCTION: Both good and bad women are mentioned in the Bible. Solomon placed a great price on a virtuous woman. His evaluation was: rubies are valuable, but virtuous women are far more valuable. (*Virtuous* means, "morally excellent, upright, righteous, moral, chaste.")

I. A VIRTUOUS WOMAN IS TRUSTWORTHY

"The heart of her husband doth safely trust in her." V. 11.

A. She will do him good.

B. He trusts her to care for the children.

C. He trusts her to be true to him.

D. He trusts her to manage the household.

E. She "worketh . . . willingly with her hands."

II. SHE IS INDUSTRIOUS

"She riseth also while it is yet night, and giveth meat to her household." V. 15.

A. She is not lazy, but is continually working to care for her family.

B. She is always on the job.

C. There is a saying that "Men work from sun to sun, but women's work is never done."

III. SHE IS BENEVOLENT

"She stretcheth out her hand to the poor; yea, she reacheth forth her hands to the needy." V. 20.

A. She is concerned about others.

B. Like Dorcas, she is a neighborhood willing worker.

C. She doesn't wait to be put on a committee.

D. Her eyes and ears are open to the needy and suffering around her.

IV. HER VALUES ARE PROPERLY PLACED

"Strength and honour are her clothing; and she shall rejoice in time to come." V. 25.

A. She is not looking for praise.

B. She knows honor is more desirable than ornaments.

C. She knows that the tinsel and artificiality of this old world is only temporary and that holiness and honor will bring rejoicing in time to come.

D. She knows ". . . her own works praise her in the gates." V. 31.

V. SHE IS WISE AND KIND

"She openeth her mouth with wisdom; and in her tongue is the law of kindness." V. 26.

A. The wisdom and advice of a good woman is invaluable.

B. Her kindness creates a gentle, warm atmosphere in the home.

VI. HER CHIEF CONCERN IS HER HOUSEHOLD

"She looketh well to the ways of her household. . . ." V. 27.

A. She doesn't seek the limelight.

B. She seeks to serve.

C. Her household is her chief concern.

VII. BECAUSE OF ALL THESE VIRTUES, HER CHILDREN WILL CALL HER BLESSED AND HER HUSBAND SHALL PRAISE HER (v. 28).

A. Her reward is in well-mannered children.

B. A husband known in the gates.

C. A well-fed, well-clothed, and well-cared-for family.

CONCLUSION: *Best of all, the Lord will call her blessed.* Her blessedness will be comparable to the following: Matthew 5:8: "Blessed are the pure in heart, for they shall see God." Matthew 5:10: "Blessed are they which are persecuted . . . for their's is the kingdom of heaven." Revelation 14:13: "Blessed are the dead which die in the Lord." Matthew 25:34: "Come, ye blessed of my Father, inherit the kingdom prepared for you from the foundation of the world."

God's Knowledge of Us

Psalm 139:1-6

INTRODUCTION: This scripture teaches us that God knows all about us.

I. DAVID DECLARED, "Thou hast searched me." He admits God's mighty searchlight was on him. He also said, "Thou understandest my thought." He knows what we are thinking about before our thoughts transfer into action. He knows them.

II. HE KNOWS HIS SHEEP. John 10:3: ". . . and he calleth his own sheep by name." It is not what we think, but what God knows. ". . . man looketh on the outward appearance, but the Lord looketh on the heart." 1 Sam. 16:7. His knowledge surpasses all human comprehension.

III. HE KNOWS MY WAYS. Job 23:10: "But he knoweth the way that I take: when he hath tried me, I shall come forth as gold." David said that God "art acquainted with all my ways." Psa. 139:3.

IV. HE KNOWS MY PATH. Prov. 4:18: ". . . the path of the just is as a shining light, that shineth more and more unto the perfect day." He knows how to guide my path and He knows the pitfalls, the snares and the traps of the enemy. "Thou compassest my path. . . ." Psa. 139:3.

V. HE KNOWETH MY NEEDS. Matt. 6:8: ". . . your Father knoweth what things ye have need of, before ye ask him." Don't worry or fret about tomorrow. He knows about all our needs. He will surely supply our needs. Phil. 4:19.

CONCLUSION: He also knows about you, sinner. You can't hide from Him. He calls for you now!

The Exercise of Faith

Eph. 2:8; 2 Peter 1:1

INTRODUCTION: In this sermon we shall consider our attitude toward this greatest of all mysteries—"faith in the soul of man." While our Lord walked among men nothing pleased Him more than seeing faith exercised.

I. WE ARE TO RECEIVE FAITH

   A. Faith is "the gift of God." Eph. 2:8. We are to obtain it. 2 Pet. 1:1.

   B. "The full assurance of faith" is received by acting in faith, on the naked promises of God.

   C. We receive from God not only joy, but joy unspeakable. Peace, yes, but peace that passeth all understanding. Love, but love that passeth knowledge. Hope, but full assurance of hope. Faith, but full assurance of faith.

   D. We are to wait upon Him until we receive the gift and obtain the faith. There is a gift of faith. 1 Cor. 12:9.

II. WE ARE TO HOLD ON TO FAITH

   A. 1 Tim. 1:19: "Holding faith, and a good conscience; which some having put away concerning faith have made shipwreck."

   B. The enemy always stretches out his hand to rob us of faith in God and His Word. We need to recognize this, and hold fast this priceless gift, *the ability to believe* absolutely and utterly in God.

   C. It would be awful to let it slip—*run out as a leaking vessel* and be empty of faith. Heb. 2:1.

   D. Let us take hold—appropriate—the "full assurance of faith."

III. WE ARE TO USE IT

A. "Have faith in God." Mark 11:22.
One man said, "Act faith—keep up repeated acts of faith."

B. Our faith should be active. It is fatal to believe that it will just come anyway. We are not just to hold it, but use it.

C. It has been said, "If the devil puts up a stone wall, we are to believe right through it." By stepping out in faith and using it, we increase our faith.

IV. CONTEND FOR THE FAITH

A. Let us "earnestly contend for the faith." Jude 3. Moffatt's translation, "Defend the faith."

B. Let us "Fight the good fight of faith," and "lay hold on eternal life." 1 Tim. 6:12.

C. ". . . we wrestle not against flesh and blood. . . ." Eph. 6:12.

D. Paul said, "I have fought a good fight, I have finished my course, *I have kept the faith.*" 2 Tim. 4:7.

V. WE ARE TO FOLLOW FAITH

A. Heb. 13:7: ". . . whose faith follow, considering the end of their conversation."

B. 1 Tim. 6:11: ". . . follow after . . . faith. . . ."

C. Receive it, hold it, follow on . . . make progress.

VI. WE ARE TO PRAY IN FAITH

A. Mark 11:24: "Therefore I say unto you, What things soever ye desire, when ye pray, *believe that ye receive them,* and ye shall have them."

B. ". . . *the prayer of faith* shall save the sick, and the Lord shall raise him up." James 5:15.

Japanese version, "The prayer that proceedeth forth from faith. . . ."

C. There is a difference between "prayer of desire" and "prayer of faith."
Prayer of desire must pass into prayer of faith before it has effect.

D. "The soul of the sluggard desireth, and hath nothing." Prov. 13:4.

E. If our prayers do not reach the faith level, the desire for prayer will vanish away.

VII. WE ARE TO BUILD UP OURSELVES IN FAITH

Jude 20: ". . . building up yourselves on your most holy faith."

A. Our foundation must be faith in God. Our singing, praying, preaching, our worship, our service, our daily work, all should be built on faith.

B. Everything we do, we must do it in faith. "Live by faith," and "walk by faith."

C. We must not build on unbelief or on suspicion or on personality, but on FAITH.

CONCLUSION: Let us exercise our faith in the promises and the power of our Lord. It pleases Him for us to have faith that "He is" and that "He is a rewarder of them that diligently seek him."

Trusting the Lord

Psalm 73:28

INTRODUCTION: This is a day when people don't know who or what to trust. But one thing is certain and sure, we can always trust in our God.

I. THIS TEXT IS A DECLARATION OF A PERSONAL TRUST.

"I have put *my trust* in the Lord. . . ." Psa. 73:28.

A. *This was not what others were doing.* Psalm 20:7: "Some trust in chariots, and some in horses. . . ." Psalm 44:6: "For I will not trust in my bow, neither shall my sword save me."

B. *BUT, "I will trust in the Lord,"* says David. It seemed simple, but it was a bold step when most were trusting in something else.

C. *It was a positive and determined trust.* There is no haphazard, wishy-washy business here. As positive as Job 13:15, "Though he slay me, yet will I trust in him." It is good to think of David, Moses, Elijah, Paul and Peter, but what about us?

II. IT IS A DECLARATION OF PUTTING TRUST IN THE RIGHT PLACE.

". . . in the Lord God," said David.

A. David knew that God had not failed his fathers. He was also willing to trust Him for He was Jehovah, the tried and the true One, the great God.

B. David also knew what it was to put his trust in man and have man to fail him. Psa. 118:8, 9: "It is better to trust in the Lord than to put confidence in man. It is better to trust in the Lord than to put confidence in princes."

C. Jeremiah 17:5: "Cursed be the man that trust-eth in man. . . ."

D. *David knew by personal experience* that to put his trust in God meant *dead bear, dead lion,* and *dead giant.*

E. *In his song of deliverance,* he says, ". . . he is a buckler to all them that trust in him." 2 Sam. 22:31.

F. Psalm 56:3: "What time I am afraid, I will trust in thee." David didn't even trust David. He trusted God.

III. IT IS A DECLARATION OF A SETTLED AND FIXED DETERMINATION.

A. *It is a bargain for keeps.* Not I might, nor maybe, nor I'll think it over. Not even, I will, but *I HAVE.* It is settled. His heart and mind have agreed. It is fixed, signed and sealed.

B. And David said, "My heart is fixed, O God, my heart is fixed. . . ." Psa. 57:7.

C. Paul declared, ". . . for I know whom I have believed, and am persuaded that he is able to keep that. . . ." 2 Tim. 1:12.

D. Where is your trust? Is it in riches, in man, in the armed might of an army, in church membership, in profession, in water baptism, in good works? The best and safest place is "in the Lord."

CONCLUSION: When we commit our way to the Lord, and trust also in Him; He shall bring it to pass. Psa. 37:5.

The Testing of Faith

James 1:12

INTRODUCTION: This text states, "Blessed is the man that endureth temptation: for when he is tried, he shall receive the crown of life, which the Lord hath promised to them that love him." Moffatt's Translation: "Blessed is he who endures under trial; for when he has stood the test, he will gain the crown of life." The devil tempts us to bring out the evil, the Lord tests to bring out the good.

In verse 2, James said, ". . . count it all joy when ye fall into divers temptations." And in verse 3, "Knowing this, that the trying of your faith worketh patience." Moffatt's Translation: "Count it as pure joy, when you encounter any sort of trial."

In 1 Peter 4:12, we are admonished to "think it not strange concerning the fiery trial which is to try you, as though some strange thing happened unto you."

And in verse 13, to "rejoice, inasmuch as ye are partakers of Christ's sufferings; that, when his glory shall be revealed, ye may be glad also with exceeding joy." Moffatt's Translation: "Do not be surprised at the ordeal that has come to test you."

1 Peter 1:7: "That the trial of your faith, being much more precious than of gold that perisheth, though it be tried with fire, might be found unto praise and honour and glory at the appearing of Jesus Christ."

I. THE TESTING OF FAITH'S DETERMINA-
TION—Ruth 1:8, 11, 12, 15.

    A. This heathen girl knew very little about God. Her life was young, fresh, full of promise and possibility. Was Naomi really trying to get them to go back or was it a "test"?

B. How many have started out with good intentions, but when trials came, turned back?

C. In verse 8, Naomi said, "Go, return each to her mother's house." She kissed them and they wept. They said, ". . . we will return with thee unto thy people." But in verse 11, Naomi said, "Turn again," to your own people. In verse 12 the same advice was given. FOUR times she said, "go your way."

D. Naomi declared, "I have no more sons." My case is hopeless. They wept again. Orpah "kissed her" and went back. But Ruth "clave unto her." Again Naomi urged her to go back to her people, ". . . thy sister in law is gone back," now you go back. It was a good chance; she had company.

But Ruth was determined, "Intreat me not to leave thee, or to return from following after thee: for whither thou goest, I will go; and where thou lodgest, I will lodge: thy people shall be my people, and thy God my God."

E. "When she saw that she was steadfastly minded to go with her, then she left speaking unto her." V. 18.

F. Ruth's faith and determination convinced Naomi that further insistence was useless. Orpah leaves behind nothing but a name like Cain, Esau, Ishmael, the Pharisee and the Prodigal Son's elder brother.

BUT RUTH chose to cleave to Naomi. Naomi says, "Go back." Surely she has been tested enough; but, *NO, THE DETERMINATION OF FAITH MUST BE TRIED. THE COST MUST BE COUNTED.* We must know that roses do not lie all along the road. There are some thorns among the roses.

II. TESTING OF FAITH'S MOTIVES—Ex. 32:7-14.

A. Moses was on the mountain receiving the law from God, but there was trouble in the valley below. He had borne the burden of their murmurings, unbelief and backslidings. They were full of idolatry and apostasy, yet he pleads for them.

B. God says, "let me alone, I will destroy this people." It is not "this" people, Moses reminds Him, but "thy" people. *HE REFUSES TO ALLOW GOD TO DISOWN THEM. What HOLY BOLDNESS!*

C. What was Moses' motive? God said, "Let me destroy them and I will make you a great nation." Moses declares, "I don't want to be great. Don't mind me. I am nobody. If you destroy them, what will happen to thy great name? Thy reputation? Thy promise? What will happen to Abraham, Isaac and Jacob. YOU promised them not me. Blot me out—but vindicate your name."

D. What a triumph of faith! God could have been testing Moses. *Would WE HAVE STOOD THE TEST?*

E. If our motives are for the good of others or for the glory of God, remember we can stand the tests. Consider David and Goliath, Hezekiah and Elijah.

III. THE TESTING OF FAITH'S PERSEVERANCE —Matt. 15:21-28.

A. Another heathen soul had seen the light by contact with some followers of Jesus. Her child was grievously vexed with a devil. "Have mercy," she cried.

B. The three negatives against her were: (1) He "answered her not a word." (2) "I am NOT sent but unto the lost sheep of the house of Israel." (3) "It is NOT meet to take the children's bread, and cast it to dogs." Many mothers would have failed.

C. He granted her request and left her as a monument and an encouragement to millions and a rebuke to unbelief. In the face of His silence, rebuke and rebuff, she still believed and persevered.

D. Afterwards she must have gloried in the testing . . . counting it joy.

POEM

It is quite easy sailing the sea in a calm
To trust in the might of Jehovah's great arm
And wondrous I find when waves swamp the boat
It takes some believing to keep things afloat.

IV. THE TESTING OF FAITH'S LIMIT—John 11:1-24.

A. God always has a deep purpose in testing. If we believe, He leads into larger believing. Mary and Martha sent Jesus word that Lazarus was dead.

B. They had faith and felt assured Jesus would get there in time. But, when He didn't . . . confusion of mind and sorrow of heart. Who could be expected to believe now?

C. Lazarus has passed the jaws of death—"Hopeless." What was His purpose in testing?

CONCLUSION: There were three lessons they learned that day. (1) Martha learned that He was the resurrection. (2) Mary learned if she would believe she would see the impossible. (3) Lazarus learned He was not only a healer, but the conqueror of death.

I Have Sinned

Luke 15:18

INTRODUCTION: ". . . by one man sin entered into the world." Rom. 5:12. ". . . all have sinned, and come short of the glory of God." Rom. 3:23. Romans 5:19: Through "one man's disobedience many were made sinners. . . ." Sin must be confessed. 1 John 1:9. 1 John 1:8: "If we say that we have no sin, we deceive ourselves, and. . . ." 1 John 1:10: "If we say that we have not sinned, we make him a liar. . . ." 1 John 3:4: ". . . sin is the transgression of the law." Proverbs 14:34: ". . . sin is a reproach to any people." Romans 6:23: ". . . the wages of sin is death. . . ."

I. PHARAOH! Ex. 9:27-34; 10:16.

    A. After God sent plagues on Pharaoh, he called Aaron and Moses and said, *"I have sinned* this time: the Lord is righteous . . . I and my people are wicked." V. 27. He asked Moses to entreat the Lord for him. He wanted Moses' prayers.

    B. But verse 34 says, ". . . he sinned yet more, and hardened his heart. . . ." Then God sent locusts. Pharaoh called Moses again and said, "I have sinned against the Lord your God, and against you. Now therefore forgive, I pray thee, my sin only this once, and intreat the Lord your God, that he may take away from me this death only."

    C. *This is a.type of person who doesn't pray until trouble comes . . . he will not pray while the sun shines.*

    D. He eventually needs help and prayer but there is no one to help. Pharaoh was buried beneath the waters of the sea.

84

II. BALAAM! Numbers 22:34.

A. Balaam said to the angel of the Lord, *"I have sinned." This type of man wants "honor" more than God's smile of approval.*

B. Jude tells of "the error of Balaam." V. 11.

C. 2 Peter 2:15 speaks of ". . . the way of Balaam."

D. Balak promised Balaam promotion to honor. His first answer was good. He made a mistake when he prayed the second time. He tried to change God for a selfish purpose. God was angry.

E. Balaam wanted to die the death of the righteous. But one must live the righteous life to die the righteous death.

III. ACHAN! Joshua 7:20.

A. *"I have sinned* against the Lord God of Israel." He was warned not to take anything out of the city. But he took the Babylonian garment, 200 shekels of silver and a wedge of gold. He hid his loot in the tent!

B. His testimony was, "I saw, I coveted, I took." He duplicated Eve's sin in the garden. Gen. 3:6. Joshua took him, his family, sheep, oxen and stoned them all to death. "He that covereth his sins shall not prosper." Prov. 28:13. Achan could not cover his sin, and he confessed too late. Sin effects more than the individual who commits it.

IV. SAUL! 1 Sam. 15:24.

A. "And Saul said unto Samuel, *I have sinned:* for I have transgressed the commandment of the Lord, and thy words: because I *feared the people,* and obeyed their voice."

B. He confessed too late. It is a sad story. 1 Sam. 15:11 states that Samuel was ". . . grieved and he cried unto the Lord all night." We should feel the burden when our families and friends sin against God.

C. 1 Sam. 26:21: "Then said Saul, *I have sinned:* return, my son David: for I will no more do thee harm, because my soul was precious in thine eyes this day: behold, I have played the fool, and have erred exceedingly." "Fools make a mock at sin. . . ." Prov. 14:9. It is foolish to treat sin lightly. It should be shunned like a vicious, venomous snake.

V. DAVID! 2 Sam. 12:13.

A. "David said unto Nathan, *I have sinned* against the Lord." He confessed in time.

B. 1 John 1:9: "If we confess our sins, he is faithful and just to forgive us our sins. . . ."

C. No matter what the sin, if we confess it, we will be forgiven, if we do not wait too late.

D. ". . . but whoso confesseth and forsaketh them [sins] shall have mercy." Prov. 28:13.

VI. JUDAS! Matt. 27:4.

A. ". . . when he saw that he was condemned, repented himself." Matt. 27:3. He brought back the thirty pieces of silver and cried in agony and despair, *"I have sinned* in that I have betrayed the innocent blood." Matt. 27:4.

B. The chief priests and elders said, "What is that to us?" In other words, it is your problem, not ours.

C. When we serve sin, we get in trouble. Satan will get us in trouble and leave us there.

VII. THE PRODIGAL SON! Luke 15:20.

A. The story is rich with meaning, love and forgiveness.

B. He came to himself. And when he did, he went back to his father's house. He confessed to him, *"I have sinned* against heaven, and in thy sight. . . ."

C. Yes, he decided to go back and make a clean confession. This is the only route of restoration.

D. ". . . whoso confesseth and forsaketh them shall have mercy." Prov. 28:13. His father welcomed him home. He gave him the best of everything.

CONCLUSION: "Come now, and let us reason together, saith the Lord: though your sins be as scarlet, they shall be as white as snow. . . ." Isa. 1:18. Thank God for this generous invitation He gives to all who have sinned.

The Tragedy of Turning Back

Psalm 78:7-11

INTRODUCTION: A quitter, a deserter, a coward is no asset to an army, to a church or to any other institution. The church especially, needs strong stalwart soldiers who will fight the good fight of faith until the end. Jesus said, "No man, having put his hand to the plough, and looking back, is fit for the kingdom of God." Luke 9:62. There are always reasons for turning back. Let us discuss examples of turning back.

I. SAUL TURNED BACK FROM FOLLOWING GOD. 1 SAM. 15:11.

   A. This same scripture says that ". . . it grieved Samuel; and he cried unto the Lord all night." 1 Sam. 15:11. How we need men like Samuel today!

   B. Saul had not performed the commandment of God. V. 11.

   C. He was stubborn and rebelled against God's will. V. 23. *He accused the people of taking the* spoil. V. 21. This is the same route Eve, Adam, Pilate and others have taken. He blamed someone else for his own sin.

   D. He rejected the Word of the Lord. V. 23.

II. ORPAH TURNED BACK. Ruth 1:14, 15.

   A. She followed Naomi a short distance from home, but turned back. She kissed her, but she turned back. Verse 14 says, "Orpah kissed her mother in law; but Ruth clave unto her."

   B. There was a lot of difference between Orpah and Ruth and between kissing and cleaving.

88

Ruth couldn't be forced to turn back. Orpah wouldn't pay the price to go on.

C. Ruth goes on, but Orpah turned back. Ruth went on to greatness, Orpah turned back to obscurity. The ties holding Orpah were too strong. She saw no extra gain by sticking with Naomi.

D. Verse 15 says, she is (1) "gone back unto her people." Kinfolk cause many to turn back. (2) She went back "unto her gods." She loved her idol gods more than she did Jehovah God and Naomi.

III. GIDEON'S MEN TURNED BACK. Judges 7:2-8.

A. "And there returned of the people twenty and two thousand; and there remained ten thousand." V. 3.

B. God told Gideon to tell the fearful and afraid to return. They had a choice to either shape up and be men or to go back. They chose the latter.

C. Then 9,700 more left because they couldn't stand the test. V. 7.

D. For every one that stayed 106 plus turned back.

E. What would be the ratio today?

IV. MANY DISCIPLES TURNED BACK. John 6:66.

A. ". . . many of his disciples went back, and walked no more with him."

B. They were offended at His words.

C. They were tested by doctrine. Paul said, ". . . the time will come when they will not endure [tolerate] sound doctrine." 2 Tim. 4:3.

D. Paul speaks of "good doctrine." 1 Tim. 4:6. He

also said, ". . . give attendance . . . to doctrine."
V. 13.

E. The beloved Apostle John said, "Whosoever transgresseth, and abideth not in the doctrine of Christ, hath not God." 2 John 9.

V. JOHN MARK TURNED BACK. Acts 15:37-41.

A. Paul and Barnabas planned a preaching mission. Barnabas wanted to take his nephew, John Mark, but Paul refused.

B. The reason: John Mark had "departed from them . . . and went not with them to the work." V. 38.

C. Was he lazy? Cowardly? Or was he just homesick? Did he depart from them because he didn't like his part in the program?

D. Perhaps the glamour had worn off. Or maybe the good times of the bright lights were calling.

E. Maybe he was tired of hearing the same two preachers all the time. It could be he had lost his "love of the truth." 2 Thess. 2:10.

F. But thank God, John Mark made a change. Later Paul said that Mark was "profitable to me [Paul] for the ministry." 2 Tim. 4:11.

VI. DEMAS TURNED BACK. 2 Tim. 4:10.

A. Paul said, "Demas hath forsaken me. . . ." This man turned his back on the greatest preacher of his day. He had rather hear worldly prattle than powerful preaching. He enjoyed playing more than praying, sensuality more than sacrifice and carefree living more than carrying the cross of Christ.

B. He "loved this present world." His love for things present outweighed his love for a guar-

90

anteed future in that heavenly world. The glitter and glamour of the present world shined brighter to him than the "Bright and Morning Star."

C. All God's children are warned against loving this present evil world. Gal. 1:4; 1 John 2:15, 16; James 4:4.

VII. LOT'S WIFE LOOKED BACK. Gen. 19:15-26.

A. She was warned by the angel, "look not behind thee. . . ." V. 17. But she rejected his advice and "looked back . . . and she became a pillar of salt." V. 26.

B. No one will ever know for sure the real reason she looked back. Perhaps she had so much of Sodom society in her system that she just couldn't be happy any other place, even in the company of heavenly angelic personalities.

C. The pull of Sodom was just too strong. She couldn't resist a last look at the Sodomite city. There was something there she still wanted. It was inbedded so deeply in her heart that neither God, man, nor angels could extract it from her.

VIII. EPHRAIM TURNED BACK. Psalm 78:9.

A. "The children of Ephraim, being armed . . . turned back in the day of battle." V. 9.

B. After all God had done for them, they turned back. This action was not calmly considered, but was a cowardly act in the day of battle.

C. *They had no excuse.* They were armed and carrying bows. The strong always becomes weak, when God is forsaken.

D. Verses 8, 10, 11 states . . .

1. Their hearts were not right.
2. Their spirits were not stedfast with God.
3. They kept not the covenant of God.
4. They refused to walk in His law.
5. They forgot His works.
6. And they forgot His wonders.

CONCLUSION: Deception is a major cause of backsliding. Isaiah 44:20 states, ". . . a deceived heart hath turned him aside [or back]." We know we are in the last days when "evil men and seducers shall wax worse and worse, deceiving, and being deceived." 2 Tim. 3:13. Let us beware of "giving heed to seducing spirits, and doctrines of devils." 1 Tim. 4:1.

Hidden Treasures

Col. 2:1-3

INTRODUCTION: According to Daniel 1:2, God has a "treasure house." But many people never get into this house. Obedience and faith will give us access to it.

Prov. 15:6: "In the house of the righteous is much treasure."

Prov. 8:21: "That I may cause those that love me to inherit substance; and I will fill their treasures."

Col. 3:3: "Ye are dead, and your life is hid with Christ in God." (Hidden treasures for hidden saints.) *Only the faithful few ever get to examine or experience God's great treasure house.*

I. THE CHRISTIAN RELIGION IS A RELIGION OF REVELATION.

    A. Jesus told Peter that "Flesh and blood hath not revealed it unto thee, but my Father. . . ." Matt. 16:17.

    1 Peter 1:12: "Which things the angels desire to look into."

    B. "I thank thee, O Father . . . because thou hast hid these things from . . . and revealed. . . ." Matt. 11:25. It takes more than worldly wisdom to understand God's will and plan. It is more than angelic power. *IT MUST BE REVEALED.*

    C. The Gospel of Christ is a hidden gospel. 2 Cor. 4:3. It is called the "mystery of the gospel." Eph. 6:19. "This is a great mystery." Eph. 5:32. Paul said, he preached "among the Gentiles the unsearchable riches of Christ; And to make all men see what is the fellowship of the mystery. . . ." Eph. 3:8, 9. Things that are a mystery to the carnal are made plain to us through Revelation.

D. In Dan. 2:22, Daniel praised God because He revealed unto him the king's dream and interpretation. "He revealeth the deep and secret things." "There is a God in heaven that revealeth secrets." V. 28. The Chaldeans said to the king, "There is not a man *upon the earth* that can shew the king's matter." V. 10. This is half truth—Daniel was on earth, but not an earthly man. He was FULL OF HEAVEN. And he, through heaven-sent revelation, revealed the mystery.

II. REVELATION BRINGS VISION.

A. Jer. 33:3: "Call unto me, and I will answer thee, and shew thee great and mighty things. . . ." The margin says, "hidden things."

B. Heb. 11:27: Moses, by faith "forsook Egypt, not fearing the wrath of the king: for he endured, as seeing him who is invisible."

C. 1 Cor. 4:1: "stewards of the mysteries of God." Definition: Managers in charge of the mysteries.

D. Paul heard "unspeakable words . . . not lawful for a man to utter." 2 Cor. 12:4.

1 Cor. 2:9, 10: "Eye hath not seen, nor ear heard. . . . But God hath revealed them unto us by his Spirit."

E. Carnal man cannot see these wonderful things nor understand them, but the Spirit reveals them to us. Our eyes see, ears hear, our hearts understand, because of the revelation of God, through heavenly vision.

III. REVELATION GIVES KNOWLEDGE!

A. Matt. 13:11 and Luke 8:10, "It is given unto you to *KNOW* the mysteries of the kingdom of heaven, but *to them* it is not given."

B. John 14:15-17: "If ye love me. . . . And I will pray the Father . . . the world cannot receive . . . because . . . but ye know him; for he dwelleth with you, and shall be in you." Rom. 8:16; 1 John 3:14; 1 John 4:13; 1 John 3:24.

C. Nicodemus said unto Jesus, "How can these things be?" John 3:9; Rom. 16:25, 26: ". . . according to the revelation of the mystery, which was *kept secret* since the world began, *But now is made manifest,* and by the scriptures of the prophets, according to the commandment of the everlasting God, made known to all nations for the obedience of faith." While the world asks *how* we answer, *"we know!"*

D. John 3:12: "If I have told you earthly things, and ye believe not, how. . . ."

E. Col. 1:26, 27: "Even the *mystery* which *hath been hid from ages* and from generations, *but now is made manifest to his saints:* To whom God would make known what is the riches of the glory of this mystery. . . ."

IV. REVELATION GIVES HEAVENLY NOURISHMENT!

A. Jesus said, "I have meat to eat that ye know not of." John 4:32.

B. Rev. 2:17: "To him that overcometh will I give to eat of the *hidden manna*."

John 6:48-63: "I am the bread of life. Your fathers did eat manna in the wilderness, and are dead. This is the bread which cometh down from heaven, that a man may eat thereof, and not die."

John 6:53: ". . . Except ye eat the flesh of the Son of man, and drink his blood, ye have no life in you."

D. "O taste and see that the Lord is good." Psa. 34:8. My words "they are spirit and they are life." John 6:63.

E. 1 Cor. 10:21: "Ye cannot drink the cup of the Lord, and the cup of devils: ye cannot be partakers of the Lord's table, and of the table of devils."

V. REVELATION BRINGS HEARTWARMING JOY.

A. "Did not our heart burn within us . . . while he opened to us the scriptures?" Luke 24:32.

B. It is "joy unspeakable. . . ." 1 Pet. 1:8.
Joy in seeing, knowing about and feeling heavenly things.

C. "Joy of the Lord is your strength." Neh. 8:10.

D. Acts 2:1-13: The apostles acted like drunken men. Yet they were eating heavenly manna and drinking heavenly wine.

CONCLUSION: All that sinners, backsliders and hypocrites will ever know of the mysteries and wonders of God will be the "pangs of conviction" and His WRATH OF JUDGMENT. "Behold . . . the goodness and severity of God." Rom. 11:22.

96

Four Great Immovables

Heb. 6:17-19

INTRODUCTION: This is a day of change, of instability. There seems to be nothing worthwhile to hold on to . . . that will be unchanged tomorrow. A day of new ideas, ideals, philosophies, and new moralities. Governments are changing, educational institutions are changing, and churches are changing, not only in theology, but in practical Christian living. Some churches are rushing about trying to change doctrines, teachings and practices so they can be relevant to contemporary situations and circumstances. But there are still some immovables. Four of them will be discussed in this sermon.

I. THE IMMOVABLE, UNCHANGABLE GOD.

A. David testified to this great truth; "Before the mountains were brought forth, or ever thou hadst formed the earth and the world, even from everlasting to everlasting, thou art God." Psa. 90:2.

B. God himself testified to it, "For I am the Lord, I change not. . . ." Mal. 3:6.

C. *The guilt of mankind* is to change this unchanging God.

   Romans 1:21-25 states, "Because that, when they knew God, they glorified him not as God, neither were thankful; but became vain in their imaginations, and their foolish heart was darkened. Professing themselves to be wise, they became fools, And changed the glory of the uncorruptible God into an image made like to corruptible man. . . ." *Every effort of man has failed,* because God is immutable, unchanging, immovable.

D. *The nature, will and attributes of God are exempt from all change.* Reason teaches us that no change is possible in God, whether of increase

97

or decrease, progress or deterioration, contraction or development.

All change must be to better or to worse. God is absolutely perfect, and no change to better is possible. Change to worse is equally inconsistent with perfection.

E. *God is immutable because He is eternal.* He has existed from eternity and will exist for eternity.

The Word says, "underneath are the everlasting arms." Deut. 33:27.

F. *God's life operates unspent; there is ever more to follow.*

THE LEGEND—stamped with the pillars of Hercules upon the coins of Spain was *"NE PLUS ULTRA"* . . . *"nothing beyond."* But when Columbus discovered America, the legend was changed to *"PLUS ULTRA"* . . . *"MORE beyond." So, it must ever be with God.* There is more beyond, and there is plenty more beyond, and there will never cease to be plenty *"more beyond."*

G. Psalm 102:25-27, "Of old hast thou laid the foundation of the earth: and the heavens are the work of thy hands. They shall perish, but thou shall endure: yea, all of them shall wax old like a garment; as a vesture shalt thou change them, and they shall be changed. But thou art the same, and thy years shall have no end."

H. James 1:17: ". . . with whom is no variableness, neither shadow of turning."

I. *God is unchanging in His omnipotence.*
"In the beginning God created the heaven and the earth." Genesis 1:1.

"Ah Lord God! behold, thou hast made the heaven and the earth by thy great power and stretched out arm, and there is nothing too hard for thee." Jer. 32:17.

98

J. *He is unchanging in His promises.*

". . . there hath not failed one word of all his good promise. . . ." 1 Kings 8:56.

K. *He is unchanging in His holiness.*

". . . Be ye holy; for I am holy." 1 Peter 1:16.

". . . ye shall be holy; for I am holy. . . ." Lev. 11:44.

II. THE WORD OF GOD IS UNCHANGEABLE.

A. "For ever, O Lord, thy word is settled in heaven." Psa. 119:89.

". . . the word of our God shall stand for ever." Isa. 40:8.

". . . my words shall not pass away." Matt. 24:35.

". . . scripture cannot be broken." John 10:35.

B. *It is POWERFUL.* "The word of God is quick, and powerful." Heb. 4:12.

". . . like as a fire . . . like a hammer that breaketh the rock in pieces." Jer. 23:29.

C. "But *HIS WORD* was in mine heart as a burning fire shut up in my bones. . . ." Jer. 20:9.

"So shall my word be that goeth forth out of my mouth: it shall not return unto me void, but it shall accomplish that which I please, and it shall prosper in the thing whereto I sent it." Isa. 55:11.

D. *It is necessary for SALVATION.*

Romans 1:16: ". . . it is the power of God unto salvation. . . ."

John 3:16; Acts 2:38; Acts 3:19; Acts 2:21; 1 John 5:1; Romans 5:1; Acts 16:31.

E. *SANCTIFICATION.*

John 17:17-19; Hebrews 2:11-13; 1 Thess. 4:3, 4; 1 Cor. 1:2; 1 Thess. 5:23.

F. *HOLY GHOST.*

> John 14:15, 16; Luke 11:3; Acts 1:4, 5; Acts 2:
> 37-39; Matt. 3:11; John 7:37-39; Acts 10:44-48;
> Acts 5:32; Acts 19:1-6.

G. *HEALING.* ". . . who healeth all thy diseases."
Psa. 103:3.

> "I am the Lord that healeth thee." Exodus 15:
> 26.

> "Is any sick among you? let him call for the elders
> . . . And the prayer of faith shall save the sick.
> . . ." James 5:14, 15.

III. JESUS CHRIST OUR LORD IS FOREVER THE SAME.

A. "Jesus Christ the same yesterday, and to day, and
for ever." Hebrews 13:8.

B. "How God anointed Jesus of Nazareth with the
Holy Ghost and with power. . . ." Acts 10:38.

> "Jesus of Nazareth, a man approved of God
> among you by miracles and wonders and signs,
> which God did by him in the midst of you, as
> ye. . . ." Acts 2:22.

C. *There are too many miracles to innumerate.*

> He healed the sick, cast devils out of the demo-
> niac, blessed little children, stilled the winds and
> waves, etc.

D. But, His ministry did not cease at the cross, nor
at the conclusion of His 40 days upon earth,
after the resurrection.

E. *He is our High Priest! He is the same Saviour
and Lord . . . now! today!*

> ". . . when he had by himself purged our sins,
> sat down on the right hand of the Majesty on
> high. . . ." Heb. 1:3.

100

F. "For Christ is not entered into the holy places made with hands, which are the figures of the true; but into heaven itself, now *to appear in the presence of God for us.*" Heb. 9:24.

G. "Seeing then that we have a great *HIGH PRIEST*, that is passed into the heavens, Jesus the Son of God, let us hold fast our profession. For we have not an high priest which cannot be touched with the feeling of our infirmities. . . ." Heb. 4:14, 15.

H. "An high priest over the house of God. . . ." Heb. 10:21.

I. "But this man, because he *continueth ever, hath an unchangeable priesthood.* Wherefore he is able to save to . . . seeing *he ever liveth* to make intercession for them." Heb. 7:24, 25.
"I am he that liveth, and was dead; and, behold, *I am alive for evermore. . . .*" Rev. 1:18.

J. "We have such an high priest, who is set on the right hand of the throne of the Majesty in the heavens; *A minister of the sanctuary,* and of the true tabernacle, which the Lord pitched, and not man." Heb. 8:1, 2.

K. *"High Priest"* . . . *"Over the house of God."*
 1. "He can be touched."
 2. "Continueth ever."
 3. "Unchangeable priesthood."
 4. "Minister of the sanctuary."
 5. "Appearing in the presence of God for us."

L. *He is our mediator.*

1 Tim. 2:5: "For there is one God, and one mediator between God and men, the man Christ Jesus."

Heb. 9:15: ". . . he is the mediator of the new testament."

101

Heb. 8:6: ". . . a more excellent ministry . . . mediator of a better covenant."

M. *He is our advocate.*

1 John 2:1: ". . . if any man sin, we have an advocate with the Father, Jesus Christ the righteous. . . ."

Berkeley: "We have a counsel for our defense. . . ." An attorney—lawyer—a defender—pleader. . . .

IV. THE CHURCH IS IMMOVABLE, IT WILL NEVER BE DEFEATED.

A. Matt. 16:18: ". . . I will build my church; and the gates of hell shall not prevail against it." The church . . . the called-out ones . . . God's visible witness in the world.

B. He will protect it, *because it is His purchased possession.* Acts 20:28. *It cost Him His life.*

C. Eph. 5:23-25 ". . . Christ is the head of the church: and he is the saviour of the body. . . . Christ also loved the church, and gave himself for it."
Col. 1:18: "And he [Christ] is the head of the body, the church. . . ."

D. 1 Cor. 12:27: "Now ye are the body of Christ, and members in particular."

E. He gave the church power to . . . (1) protect itself by its gifts, 1 Cor. 12:4-11, 28-31; (2) propagate its message by its ministries, Eph. 4:11-13; and (3) emanate its influence by its fruit, Gal. 5:22, 23.

CONCLUSION: In a world of instability, uncertainty and even disaster these great immovables are stronger than the Rock of Gibralter, brighter than the brightest sun, and more powerful than any force in this whole wide world.

Where Are You at Calvary?

Luke 23:33-38

INTRODUCTION: There is a song that contains these words, "Were you there when they crucified my Lord?" This sermon is a study of the different groups present during the crucifixion of Christ.

I. THE SOLDIERS.

    A. They clad Him in a robe . . . spat in His face . . . put a crown of thorns on His head . . . mocked Him . . . and nailed Him to a tree. They taunted Him, by saying, *"If thou be the King of the Jews, save thyself."*

    B. The devil said to Jesus, *"If thou be the Son of God,* command that these stones be made bread." Matt. 4:3.

    C. We read further that ". . . sitting down they watched him there." Matt. 27:36. We say they were hard-hearted . . . true! But what about those today who watch Him in sermon, song, testimony . . . and just go on their way.

    D. Then, "they gambled for His robe." (They wanted His robe, but they needed the man.) We are all "Soldiers of the Cross," or "Soldiers at the Cross." There is a big difference. . . . Some have given all for "the man Christ Jesus." 1 Tim. 2:5. Some have gambled away their day of grace. What kind of soldier are you?

II. THE SECOND GROUP "PASSED BY WAGGING THEIR HEADS." They also "reviled him." Matt. 27:39.

103

A. They didn't crucify Him . . . they just wagged their heads and went on their way.

B. It's fashionable these days to "wag" the head at Calvary . . . the Blood . . . the Resurrection . . . and the Second Coming.

The Scriptures reveal three (3) things about this group.

First, they misquoted the claims of our Lord.

They said, "Thou that destroyeth the temple and buildeth it in three days, save Thyself. He did not say He would destroy the temple built by the hands of men, when He said, ". . . destroy this temple, and in three days I will raise it up." John 2:19. He was speaking of His body.

This is the group that twists the Scriptures to fit their own unscriptural arguments.

Second, they minimized His death.

". . . save thyself," they said, not knowing the significance of the cross. Matt. 27:40.

They didn't know He "must needs have suffered." Acts 17:3. And that He came "to seek and to save that which was lost." Luke 19:10. Christ taught, "For whosoever will save his life shall lose it." Matt. 16:25.

This group is of the anti-slaughterhouse religion philosophy; that say we can save ourselves by good works and that the blood religion is repulsive to rational right-thinking people.

Third, they said,

"If thou be the Son of God, come down from the cross." V. 40.

They challenged His Sonship—His Deity. Followers of this group are still with us. He didn't come down from *the cross,* but He will come down from *His throne* on that great day.

III. THE THIRD GROUP . . . CHIEF PRIESTS . . .
SCRIBES . . . ELDERS. Matt. 27:41-43. The religious leaders of that day.

A. *They mocked Him.* V. 41.

There were scoffers and mockers in that day,
and there are ". . . in the last days scoffers. . . ."
2 Pet. 3:3, 4.

B. *They denied He had power to save Himself.*
"He saved others; himself he cannot save." He
could have called 12 legions of angels to free him.
Matt. 26:53. One angel slew 185,000 men. 2
Kings 19:35.

C. *They rejected His Kingship over Israel.*
"If he be the King of Israel, let him 'NOW'
come down. . . ." They evidently did not understand or else did not believe their prophet Isaiah.
Isa. 9:6, 7.

D. *For outward show, they made their belief in His
Kingship contingent on His coming down from
the cross.* V. 42. ". . . If he be the King of
Israel, let him come down from the cross, and
we will believe him."

E. *They intimated that God had rejected Him.*
"He trusted in God; let him deliver him 'NOW',
if he will have him." V. 43.

F. Do you stand with this crowd at calvary? They
are just as much lost as the soldiers, head-wag-
gers, etc.

IV. THE FOURTH GROUP IS THE GENERAL
CROWD, TERMED SIMPLY, "THE PEOPLE."
"And the people stood beholding." Luke 23:35.

A. Most people are in this class. They didn't "crucify Him" . . . "wag their heads" . . . or "revile
Him" . . . they just looked and *did nothing.*

105

"How shall we escape, if we neglect. . . ." Heb. 2: 3.

B. It is added, ". . . [they] smote their breasts, and returned." Luke 23:48. It is possible to go this far, yet be lost. The Publican "smote upon his breast," but he went further by praying, "God be merciful to me a sinner." Luke 18:13.

V. FIFTH, THE CENTURION, WENT FURTHER.

A. *He "feared greatly."* Matt. 27:54. But, ". . . the devils also believe, and tremble." James 2:19.

B. Next, he said, ". . . *certainly this was a righteous man.*" Luke 23:47.

C. *He believed in His deity* . . . he said, "Truly this was the Son of God." Matt. 27:54.

D. *And finally, He glorified God.* It is possible to say "Lord, Lord," and yet be told "I never knew you." Matt. 7:21-23.

VI. SIXTH, THE PENITENT THIEF WHO WAS SAVED AT CALVARY. Luke 27:39-43.

A. *What a picture!* The Son of God dying between two sons of men; between heaven and earth, the handiwork of His creation; a lamb, between two wolves, the innocent dying for the guilty, the sinless for the sinful, the clean for the unclean.

B. *There were three on crosses that day.* One was dying in sin, one dying to sin, but on the middle cross, the sinless one was dying for sin; the sin and sins of all humanity.

C. It has been said, *"one was saved that none may despair,* and *only one* that none may presume."

D. It has also been said, He will save unto the uttermost, and that He will save unto the guttermost. Heb. 7:25; Luke 8:27-36.

VII. AND LAST, ALL WHO PLUNGE BENEATH THE FOUNTAIN FILLED WITH BLOOD, BELONG TO THIS GROUP.

A. "And there followed him *a great company of people,* and of women, which also bewailed and lamented him." Luke 23:27.

B. It is further stated, "And all his acquaintance, and the *women that followed him* from Galilee, stood afar off, beholding these things." V. 49.

C. These are the ones who loved Him; His acquaintance, and the women who followed Him.

D. Are we following Him? Most people are rejecting Him, or doubting Him, or just looking on, or wagging their heads, or reviling Him, or misquoting His claims, or gambling for His robe, or challenging His Deity, or mocking Him, or denying His power to save. Some are guilty of one of these attitudes, some several, and some, all of them.

CONCLUSION: We "who sometimes were far off are made nigh by the blood of Christ." Eph. 2:13. "I am crucified with Christ," said Paul. Gal. 2:20. Our sins were there on the cross with Him. But thank God, He "put away sin by the sacrifice of himself." Heb. 9:26.

God's Appointments

Hebrews 9:27

INTRODUCTION: We have many appointments in life, but none are as important as the ones God has made for us. We can and do break many earthly appointments, but God's appointments must be met. This sermon deals with four of them. If we accept the first two, we need not worry about the other two. But, if we do not, it will be terrible to meet the last two appointments.

I. HE HAS APPOINTED US TO OBTAIN SALVATION.

    A. 1 Thess. 5:9: "For God hath not appointed us to wrath, but to obtain salvation by our Lord Jesus Christ." He hath appointed, or arranged, or made a way for us to obtain salvation.

    B. Titus 2:11: "For the grace of God that bringeth salvation hath appeared to all men."

    C. John 3:17: "For God sent not his Son into the world to condemn the world; but that the world through him might be saved."

    D. Matt. 1:21: ". . . she shall bring forth a son, and thou shalt call his name Jesus: for he shall save his people from their sins."

    E. John 1:29: "Behold the Lamb of God, which taketh away the sin of the world."

    F. Romans 10:13: "For whosoever shall call upon the name of the Lord shall be saved."

G. Luke 19:9: "And Jesus said unto him, This day is salvation come to this house."

II. HE HAS APPOINTED US A KINGDOM.

A. In Luke 22:29 Jesus said, "And I appoint unto you a kingdom, as my Father hath appointed unto me."
This certainly must be twofold. There is a kingdom now. We are born into the kingdom. We are heirs of a kingdom to come.

B. Matt. 5:5: "Blessed are the meek: for they shall inherit the earth."

C. Rev. 5:10 tells us of a day when we will be kings and priests and reign on the earth. Rev. 20:6 tells us that we will be priests and shall reign with him for 1,000 years.

D. That will be our day. "In that day shall there be upon the bells of the horses, holiness unto the Lord." Zech. 14:20. Also on the pots and pans in Jerusalem. The righteous shall reign and we will put down evil and corruption.

E. Then the eternal kingdom will come. Rev. 21 and 22.

III. IT IS APPOINTED UNTO MAN TO DIE!

A. Heb. 9:27: "And as it is appointed unto men once to die, but after this the judgment."

B. Job 14:1, 2: "Man that is born of a woman is of few days, and full of trouble. He cometh forth like a flower, and is cut down. . . ."

C. James 4:14: "Whereas ye know not what shall be on the morrow. For what is your life? It is even a vapour, that appeareth for a little time, and then vanisheth away."

D. Men may turn the first two down, but not this one.

E. All must die! The rich man with his purple robe and riches died, "And in hell he lift up his eyes." Luke 16:23.

F. The rich man with barns filled died. Luke 12: 16-21. Lazarus—poor and despised—died. Luke 16: 22.

G. It comes to all alike. ALL MUST DIE. All races, all creeds, all colors. We can be ready for it. Paul said, "For I am now ready to be offered, and the time of my departure is at hand. I have fought a good fight, I have finished my course, I have kept the faith: Henceforth there is laid up for me a crown of righteousness, which the Lord, the righteous judge, shall give me at that day: and not to me only, but unto all them also that love his appearing." 2 Tim. 4:6-8. ". . . they that were ready went in . . . and the door was shut." Matt. 25:10.

IV. HE HAS APPOINTED A DAY OF JUDGMENT.

". . . but after this the judgment." Heb. 9:27.

A. Acts 17:31: "Because he hath appointed a day, in the which he will judge the world in righteousness by that man w h o m he hath ordained. . . ."

B. As all sinners must meet the appointment of death, so must they meet this judgment day appointment. Hebrews 2:3: "How shall we escape, if we neglect so great salvation."

C. Eccl. 12:13, 14: "Let us hear the conclusion of the whole matter: Fear God. . . . For God shall bring every work into judgment. . . ."

Eccl. 11:9: "Rejoice, O young man, in thy youth; and let thy heart cheer thee in the days of thy youth, and walk in the ways of thine heart, and in the sight of thine eyes: but know thou, that for all these things God will bring thee into judgment."

110

Revelation 20:11-15: "And I saw a great white throne, and him that sat on it, from whose face the earth and the heaven fled away; and there was found no place for them. And I saw the dead, small and great, stand before God; and *the books were opened:* and *another book* was opened, which is *the book of life:* and the dead were judged out of those things which were written in the books, according to their works. And the sea gave up the dead which were in it; and death and hell delivered up the dead which were in them: and they were judged every man according to their works. And death and hell were cast into the lake of fire. This is the second death. And whosoever was not found written in the book of life was cast into the lake of fire."

CONCLUSION: What will your decision be? Accept His salvation and the kingdom He has appointed unto you. Do it today!

The Cost of Prayer

Daniel 10:14

INTRODUCTION: This was the climax of Daniel's prayer life. For three weeks he had waited for an answer. It came in wonderful fullness. Daniel received the answer to his prayer and it meant victory for God and defeat for Satan. How are we to get a similar answer? It is no easy thing to pray and to pray through like Daniel. How did he reach this point? In his life there were three outstanding features showing the secret of his victory.

I. THERE WAS NO COMPROMISE WITH SELF. Daniel 1:8

    A. Rigid discipline, close adherence to what was right marked his attitude. He "purposed in his heart that he would not," was the keynote of his life. ". . . the spirit indeed is willing, but the flesh is weak." Matt. 26:41. Flesh warreth against spirit. Rom. 7:23; Gal. 5:17. ". . . deny himself." Luke 9:23.

    B. It was said of old George Fox, the Quaker, by the soldiers who guarded him in the castle of Scarborough that "he was as stiff as a tree, and as pure as a bell: we could never bow him." The same is true in early years, as well as in later years.

II. HE HAD NO UNWORTHY RELATIONS WITH KING OR STATE.

    A. With Daniel there was first no fear of royal power. Like Moses, "not fearing the wrath of the king. . . ." Heb. 11:27.

    B. No desire for world's rewards. Like Elijah, self-interest was unknown to him.

III. HE WAS NOT GUILTY OF UNFAITHFUL-NESS TO GOD. Dan. 6:4-10

A. Daniel prayed when it was against a royal decree.

B. He would not defile himself with the king's meat.

C. He refused to do anything wrong to enhance his position.

By a consideration of these three points can we calculate the cost of prayer and of receiving answers to prayer.

There can be no slackness in regard to our own lives. How easy it is to resort to self-vindication. The cost of being men and women of prayer is, in the first instance, shown by honest dealing with what we know to be our own weaknesses and failures. There are three things which we must know.

1. The realization of the imperativeness of prayer.

2. A conviction of the cost of prayer. It is hard work to travail in prayer. Praying through may cost some sacrifices.

3. Knowledge of the power of prayer. Personal communication. Contact God in behalf of others.

CONCLUSION: We must pray for strength and guidance to stay close to God and to help others.

Gethsemane

Matt. 26:36-46

INTRODUCTION: Gethsemane is where the greatest battle of all time was fought and won—just a little ways out of Jerusalem. The word *Gethsemane* means "olive press." Gethsemane is located across the Brook Kidron, near the foot of the Mount of Olives.

In the garden the first man fell through yielding to the wicked one; in a garden the second Adam conquered by yeilding to the Holy One.

The place called Gethsemane was to Him . . .

I. A PLACE OF HEAVINESS

He "began to be sorrowful and very heavy." Who can tell the weight of the burden that was laid on Him.

Isaiah 53:6: "The Lord . . . laid on him the iniquity of us all." What a burden. All the sins of the world on Him.

When we think our burdens are heavy, think of Gethsemane.

II. A PLACE OF INTENSE SUFFERING

He said, "My soul is exceeding sorrowful unto death." Mark 14:34.

OUR SUBSTITUTE: He stood between God and man. 1 Peter 3:18: "Christ . . . once suffered for sins, the just for the unjust, that he might. . . ."

He was in deep sympathy with the holiness of God, and the helplessness of man. May we today, see His suffering, and when we think we are suffering, THINK OF GETHSEMANE.

114

III. A PLACE OF SOLEMN LONELINESS.

He told His disciples to watch: "What, could ye not watch with me one hour?" The tender heart of the man of sorrow yearned for fellowship, but they "could not." They slept during his agony, while his "sweat was as it were great drops of blood. . . ."

He looked but there was none to help. Psalm 69:20: "I looked for some to take pity . . . and for comforters, but I found none." When you feel forsaken, lonely, and sad, REMEMBER GETHSEMANE.

IV. A PLACE OF AGONIZING PRAYER

He "fell on his face, and prayed, saying, O my Father, if it be possible, let this cup pass from me." He prayed the third time saying the same words. Matt. 26:39-44.

Heb. 5:7: "He . . . offered up prayers and supplications with strong crying and tears." This awful cup contained desertion and death.

The great mystery—"Behold, what . . . love. . . ." 1 John 3:1.

V. A PLACE OF ENTIRE RESIGNATION

". . . nevertheless not as I will, but as thou wilt." Matt. 26:39.

My will, not thine, opened the floodgate of sin in the first garden, and turned man out of paradise.

The second man's "not my will, but thine . . ." opened a flood of righteousness upon the world.

In the garden and in the wilderness, while being tempted of Satan, He was as firm and solid as a mountain.

It is true that the "spirit indeed is willing, but the flesh is weak." But Christ never yielded to the flesh.

We will be as strong to resist evil, in proportion as we are willing to resign to the complete will of God.

115

In every crisis, trial or experience, let us RE-
MEMBER GETHSEMANE AND SAY, "not my
will, but thine, be done."

VI. A PLACE OF SPECIAL SUCCOR

Succor means "To aid, help, assist, comfort or deliver or rescue."

Luke 22:43: ". . . there appeared an angel unto
him . . . strengthening him."

The place of entire surrender to the whole will of
God means help and comfort for every troubled
soul.

Paul says in 2 Corinthians 12:9, ". . . will I rather
glory in my infirmities, *that* the power of Christ may
rest upon me."

The angel of sufficiency will minister strength in
our weakness. My Lord declared to Paul, "My grace
is sufficient." 2 Cor. 12:9.

In Christ's greatest trial, there was an angel to
strengthen Him. Matt. 4:11. When we suffer in trials, remember He has gone this way before.

VII. A PLACE OF HEARTLESS BETRAYAL

Betrayed by the one He chose to follow Him. (Kissed
Him while the sweat was still on His brow.)

Christ had just taken man's place. All the thanks
He got was hypocritical salutation, condemnation
and death.

It is possible to play the Judas while sitting at the
Lord's table.

CONCLUSION: Do we appreciate the sacrifice He made
for us. In the hour of heaviness, suffering, loneliness,
agony of prayer, betrayal and resisting evil to make the
complete surrender, REMEMBER GETHSEMANE!

The Cross of Christ

Galatians 6:14

INTRODUCTION: The cross is a symbol of shame. The word *cross* comes from the Latin word *crux,* which means "cross, torture." *This instrument of shameful death* has become the emblem of Christianity. *But, cross means much more* than an emblem around the neck, on the walls of homes, churches, and on tombstones. The real meaning of the cross is suffering, torture, inhuman treatment, ignominy and reproach.

I. FIRST, LET US CONSIDER THE CRUELTY OF THE CROSS.

   A. *It was the most brutal, inhuman act of punishment for criminals.* Primarily, it was reserved by the Romans for slaves. This kind of death was accursed by Jews. Deut. 21:23. The New Testament says, "Cursed is every one that hangeth on a tree." Gal. 3:13.

   B. The crucifixion of Christ was the most shameful, despicable act in human history. To understand this fact you only need to look at (1) His betrayal, (2) His illegal trial, (3) falsewitnesses, (4) shameful treatment, and finally (5) His ignominous death.

      1. He was betrayed by one of His own. Matt. 27:47-50.

      2. He was falsely accused. Matt. 26:59, 60.

      3. He was illegally tried and sentenced. John 18:28-31; Luke 23:13-24.

      4. *Pilate's testimony* should have convinced them of His innocency. "I find no fault in this man." Luke 23:4.

      5. *Pilate's wife's testimony* should have had ef-

117

fect on him and his associates. She told him to "Have . . . nothing to do with that just man . . . I have suffered many things . . . in a dream because of him." Matt. 27:19.

6. Judas testified, "I have betrayed the innocent blood." Matt. 27:4.

7. His disciples "forsook him, and fled." Matt. 26:56.

8. *His enemies.* "He . . . despised and rejected of men." Isa. 53:3. They plucked out His beard, spat in His face, smote Him, mocked Him, stripped Him, and scourged Him, put a crown of thorns on His head and nailed Him to a cross.

9. *His heavenly Father* momentarily forsook Him. He was "smitten of God, and afflicted." Isa. 53:4. ". . . it pleased the Lord to bruise him." Isa. 53:10. In that awful moment (exhausted, bleeding, dying) He cried out, "My God, my God, why hast thou forsaken me?" Mark 15:34.

10. *Think of it!* (1) The "fury and scorn" of men was turned against Him. (2) He was "smitten and bruised" by His heavenly Father.

11. *God loved His Son!* But, He "so loved the world" that He gave His Son to die for its sins. His death was not only a manifestation of love, but also a manifestation of divine justice against sin. ". . . the Lord hath laid on him the iniquity of us all." Isa. 53:6. Christ became the sin offering for man.

12. ". . . he appeared to put away sin by the sacrifice of himself." Heb. 9:26. ". . . he . . . offered one sacrifice for sins for ever." Heb. 10:12.

118

13. John said, "Behold the Lamb of God [the sacrifice], which taketh away the sin of the world." John 1:29.

14. He bore "our sins in his own body on the tree. . . ." 1 Peter 2:24. "Christ . . . suffered for sins, the just for the unjust, that he might bring us to God." 1 Pet. 3:18. "Who did no sin, neither was guile found in his mouth." 1 Pet. 2:22.

15. The sinless one died for sinful sinners. The master became the slave. The guiltless became the guilty. The sinless One became or was made sin for us. ". . . one died for all . . . he died for all." 2 Cor. 5:14, 15. He was "made a curse." Gal. 3:13.

16. ". . . he humbled himself, and became obedient unto death, even. . . ." Phil. 2:8. He "endured the cross, despising the shame." Heb. 12:2.

17. The question could well be asked of Paul, "Do you mean you glory in Christ's death on the cross?" Without question his answer would be, "But God forbid that I should glory, save in the cross of. . . ."

II. SECOND, LET US CONSIDER THE CLAIMS OF THE CROSS

A. *It claims our submission to and our acceptance of its efficacious remedy for sin.*

1. ". . . without shedding of blood is no remission" of sins. Heb. 9:22.

2. ". . . for there is none other name under heaven given among men, whereby we must be saved." Acts 4:12.

3. "But if we walk in the light . . . the blood of Jesus Christ his Son cleanseth us. . . ." 1 John 1:7.

119

4. "If we confess our sins . . . cleanse us from all" sin. 1 John 1:9. ". . . Unto him that loved us, and washed us from our sins. . . ." Rev. 1:5.

5. His death, His blood is the only remedy for sin. There is no other.

B. *It claims our dedicated adherence to its eternal purpose.*

   1. Paul testified, "God forbid that I should glory, save . . ." (text). He could have gloried in education, lineage, religious training, etc. But for him to live was Christ and Him crucified.

   2. We no longer have to waint on the outside earth was to reconcile men to God. Man was estranged, alienated, cut off from God.

     Christ "made peace through the blood of his cross, by him to reconcile all things unto himself." Col. 1:20.

     For "when we were enemies, we were reconciled to God by the death of his Son." Rom. 5:10. ". . . far off are made nigh by the blood of Christ." Eph. 2:13.

   3. Heb. 2:17 states, "that he might be a merciful and faithful high priest in things pertaining to God, to make reconciliation for the sins of the people."

   4. The central theme of our concern must be to reconcile men to God; to bring them into peaceful relationship with Him through the Gospel.

   5. 2 Cor. 5:20 says, "we are ambassadors for Christ . . . we pray you in Christ's stead, be ye reconciled to God."

   6. Paul gloried in the cross because of its effects in reconciling lost men to God.

C. *The cross claims total commitment of our lives in loyal sacrifice and suffering.*

1. Rom. 12:1: "I beseech you therefore, brethren, by the mercies of God, that ye present your bodies a living sacrifice . . . unto God."

2. "He that saith he abideth in him ought himself also so to walk, even as he walked." 1 John 2:6.

3. ". . . ye are partakers of Christ's sufferings." 1 Pet. 4:13.

4. Gal. 2:20: "I am crucified with Christ. . . ." Col. 3:3: "For ye are dead, and your life is hid with Christ in God."

   Rom. 6:6: "our old man is crucified with him. . . ."

5. Paul declared he wanted to know Christ in "the fellowship of his sufferings." Phil. 3:10.

6. It takes Gethsemane and Calvary experiences to say, "Not my will, but thine, be done."

   "If we suffer. . . ." 2 Tim. 2:12.

III. THIRD, LET US CONSIDER THE CHALLENGE OF THE CROSS

A. Since we are reconciled to God by the cross, we have peace (Rom. 5:1; John 14:27; Phil. 4:7) and joy (Rom. 14:17; 1 Peter 1:8; Acts 13:52). *We are challenged to first of all worship God in spirit and in truth.*

1. The middle wall of partition is broken down.
   We are redeemed. 1 Pet. 1:18, 19.
   We are free. John 8:32, 36.
   We are sons. John 1:12.

2. We no longer have to wait on the outside for a priest to minister. He (Christ) is our High Priest. We "come boldly unto the throne of grace." Heb. 4:16.

121

3. *We worship in prayer.* "Our Father which art in heaven, Hallowed. . . ." Luke 11:2.

4. *We worship in reading the Word.* Psa. 119: 105; 2 Tim. 2:15.

5. *We worship in "singing and making melody"* in our hearts to the Lord. Eph. 5:19.

6. Examples of worship.
   In Acts 3:8, the lame man worshiped and praised God.
   The demoniac—sitting at His feet. Luke 8:35.
   The woman's tears. She brought ointment. Washed His feet with tears. Wiped them with the hairs of her head. Kissed His feet and anointed them. Luke 7:38.

B. *We are challenged to work for the Master.*

1. Why stand ye idle? The fields are white to harvest. Matt. 20:6; John 4:35.

2. We are laborers together with God. Christ told the seven churches, "I know thy works." Rev. 2:2.

3. He said, "I must work the works of him that sent me." John 9:4.

C. *We are challenged and commissioned to witness.*

1. Mark 16:15, 16; Matt. 28:19; Acts 1:8 and 5:42.

2. ". . . they went forth, and preached every where, the Lord working. . . ." Mark 16:20.

3. ". . . they that were scattered abroad went every where preaching the word." Acts 8:4.

4. Philip told Nathanael, "Come and see." John 1:46.

5. The woman at the well said, "Come, see a man." John 4:29.

6. Andrew told Peter, "We have found the Messias." John 1:41.

CONCLUSION: "I will make you fishers of men." Matt. 4:19. This is the *greatest call* that can come to man. It is the *highest honor* that will ever be bestowed upon him. If faithfully pursued it will bring the *greatest reward*.

"Must Jesus bear the cross alone and all the world go free; No, there's a cross for everyone, and there's a cross for me."

Who Cares If I Go to Hell?

"No man cared for my soul." Psa. 142:4.

INTRODUCTION: This question is often asked by those who feel the world is caving in on them. But, there is someone who cares. The disciples asked a similarly foolish question when their ship was being tossed and driven by a tempestuous wind on the sea of Galilee; "Master, carest thou not that we perish?" Mark 4:38. Jesus always cares.

Eze. 33:11: ". . . I have no pleasure in the death of the wicked . . . turn ye from your evil ways; for why will ye die. . . ."

John 6:37: ". . . him that cometh to me I will in no wise cast out."

Luke 15:10: "Likewise, I say unto you, *there is joy in the presence* of the angels of God over one sinner that repenteth."

I. *GOD THE FATHER CARES.*

    A. "The Lord is not slack . . . not willing that any should perish. . . ." 2 Peter 3:9.

    B. He gave His Son to die for our sins. John 3:16, 17. "Let the wicked forsake his way, and . . . he will abundantly pardon." Isa. 55:7.

    C. "Look unto me, and be ye saved. . . ." Isa. 45:22.

II. *THE HOLY GHOST CARES.*

    A. ". . . the Spirit and the bride say, Come." Rev. 22:17.

    B. ". . . when he is come, he will reprove the world of sin. . . ." John 16:7, 8.

C. ". . . the Holy Ghost saith, To day if ye will hear his voice, Harden not your hearts. . . ." Heb. 3:7, 8.

III. *JESUS CHRIST CARES.*

A. "Come unto me . . . and I will give you rest. . . ." Matt. 11:28-30.

B. "For the Son of man is come to seek and to save that which was lost." Luke 19:10.

C. "If any man thirst, let him come unto me. . . ." John 7:37-39.

IV. *CHRISTIANS CARE.*

A. They are praying for you. You are in their prayers every day.

B. They are ready to help you get to God.

C. They pay tithes so the gospel can be preached to you.

V. *THE LOST IN HELL CARE.*

A. The rich man in Luke 16 was concerned about his five brothers.

B. Send Lazarus to my five brothers, lest they come to this place of torment.

C. The rich man cared but he waited too late.

CONCLUSION: We must tell sinners that God, Christ, the Holy Ghost and the church cares for their souls. We should also express our own personal concern about their eternal destiny.

Contrast of Carnal and Spiritual Christians

Rom. 8:6

INTRODUCTION: The spiritual Christian takes a straight course, while the carnal Christian follows a wavering line. "A double minded man is unstable in all his ways." James 1:8.

I. *THE CARNAL LIFE IS A LIFE OF UNCEASING CONFLICT.*

A. Rom. 7:22, 23: "For I delight in the *law of God* after the *inward man:* But I see *another law* in my members, warring against the *law of my mind,* and bringing me into captivity to the *law of sin* which is in my members."

B. *Notice the words: "law of God after the inward man, another law, warring, CAPTIVITY, the law of sin."*

C. Gal. 5:17: "For the flesh lusteth against the Spirit, and the Spirit against the flesh: and these are contrary the one to the other: so that ye cannot do the things that ye would."

D. Paul declared, there is "one law" warring against "another law" in the same personality. (EXAMPLE: Ishmael and Isaac in the same house. Gen. 21:9-14.) Part of man serves one law, and part another. He wants to do right, but another law is warring against him.

E. *This is the language of conflict. Two forces "contrary" to each other warring to gain control over the entire personality. Two natures, divine and fleshly engaged in deadly warfare.*

F. When the spiritual gains the victory, the believer

enjoys momentary joy, peace and rest. When the flesh gains victory, there is doubt, gloom, unrest, distress, down in the dumps and discouragement because flesh has won a victory.

G. ILLUSTRATIONS:

A mother told her six-year-old boy not to go off. He went anyway. When she questioned him, he said, "It's this way, Mother. As I stood there in the road thinking about it, Jesus pulled on one leg and the devil pulled on the other. And the devil pulled the hardest." A Christian must not yield to wrong no matter how hard the pull.

A little boy pushed another boy in a ditch and spit on him. His mother asked him why he did it. His answer was, "The devil told me to push him in the ditch, but spitting on him was my idea." We cannot blame the devil for all our acts. Some are our ideas.

H. CONFLICT is the experience of all Christians, but the yielding and giving Satan victory is the experience of the carnal Christian.

II. *THE SPIRITUAL CHRISTIAN HAS A LIFE OF ABIDING PEACE.*

A. ". . . to be spiritually minded is life and peace." Rom. 8:6. "There is therefore now no condemnation to them. . . ." Rom. 8:1.

B. John 14:27: "Peace I leave with you, my peace I give unto you. . . ."

C. "And the peace of God, which passeth all understanding, shall keep. . . ." Phil. 4:7.

D. John 16:33: "These things I have spoken unto you, that in me ye might have peace. In the world ye shall have tribulation: but be of good cheer; I have overcome the world."

Rom. 5:1: "Therefore being justified by faith, we have peace with God through our Lord Jesus Christ."

E. This does not mean there is no conflict for the Spirit-filled Christian, for his life will be filled with spiritual battles. But through all his conflicts, there is a deep abiding peace and assurance.

F. It means his communion with the Father is unmarred by the gnawing consciousness of soiled hands, (Job 17:9: ". . . he that hath clean hands shall be stronger and stronger") or by the pricking of a wounded conscience, or by condemnation of an accusing heart.

G. There is blessed peace, deep joy, and satisfying rest. Dark days will come, but we have the bright and *Morning Star*. Waves will roll high, but we have the *Master* on board. Temptations will arise, but we have the *Conqueror*.

III. *THE CARNAL LIFE IS A LIFE OF REPEATED DEFEAT.*

A. Rom. 7:15: "For that which I do I allow not: for what I would, that do I not; but what I hate, that do I."
Rom. 7:19: "For the good that I would I do not: but the evil which I would not, that I do."

B. This shows an attempt to live the holy life, but it is surcharged with the atmosphere of deadly defeat, a defeat so overpowering as to bring forth a cry for deliverance.
Rom. 7:24: "O wretched man that I am! who shall deliver me from the body of this death?"

C. The carnal man is haunted by defeat, both commission and omission and it robs him of sleep. He is frustrated by temper, anger, fretting, worry, murmuring, pride, selfishness, malice, unfaithfulness, worldliness, evil speaking, bitterness, jealousy, envy, quarreling, hatred, and in fact by all the works of the Old Man.

D. It spoils his life and affects his family and his friends. The trouble is not the will. It was sincere at first. He wanted to do good, but evil was present to overpower him.

IV. *THE SPIRITUAL LIFE IS A LIFE OF ABIDING VICTORY.*

A. "For the law of the Spirit of life in Christ Jesus hath made me free from the law of sin and death." Rom. 8:2.

B. 1 Cor. 15:57: "But thanks be to God, which giveth us the victory through our Lord Jesus Christ."

C. Rom. 8:37: "Nay, in all these things we are more than conquerors through him that loved us."

D. 2 Cor. 2:14: "Now thanks be unto God, which always causeth us to triumph in Christ."

E. The spiritual Christian has only one master; he has perfect freedom in Christ.

F. What words! "Victory," "triumph," "conqueror!" It is not just *victories,* but *VICTORY!* This victory is not just intermittent, but habitual—"always!" And, in all places, under all circumstances, at all times, in all things, we triumph in Christ Jesus. ". . . God is able to make *all grace* abound toward you; that ye, always have *all sufficiency* in *all things,* may. . . ." 2 Cor. 9:8.

G. The carnal man is under the power of the law of sin, but the spiritual man is under the power and influence of the Spirit of God. It is a life of *VICTORY.*

129

Rom. 8:2: "For the law of the Spirit of life in Christ Jesus hath made me free from the law of sin and death."

H. Victorious—triumph—freedom—abounding.

V. *THE CARNAL LIFE IS A LIFE OF PROTRACTED INFANCY.*

A. *The carnal Christian never grows up.* He remains stunted and dwarfed. A babe in Christ. 1 Cor. 3:1, 2: "And I, brethren, could not speak unto you as unto spiritual, but as unto carnal, even as unto babes in Christ. I have fed you with milk, and not with meat: for hitherto ye were not able to bear it, *neither yet now are ye able.*"

B. *The Corinthian church should have been grown* . . . strong meat-eaters. Instead they were weak milk-drinking infants. Babies and babyhood are wonderful, but if a child does not grow in mind and body, parents are hurt and embarrassed.

C. Marks of an infant. (1) It cannot serve itself. (2) It depends on others. (3) It absorbs attention. It must be the center of attraction. (4) It is governed by its feelings. If all goes well—smiles. When things go against it—frowns.

D. Hebrews 5:12-14: It was time for these Christians to teach. They were still being taught. They could not receive nor impart the deep things of God. They esteemed lightly the wisdom of God, but esteemed highly the wisdom of men. They believed the word of man, rather than the Word of God. They were substituting fodder for food. They were trying to satisfy their hunger on husks . . . on the world's trash instead of heaven's treasures.

E. Consequently they were babes—weak, puny, emaciated, professors of religion. They looked to human teachers for nourishment and gulped down anything. Babies will eat anything and everything. They were spiritual parasites, living on predigested foods, therefore, they were underfed and anemic.

F. In this weakened condition, they were open to all forms of disease. They were susceptible to all kinds of false teaching and false doctrine. The carnal Christian is also easy prey for temper, pride, impurity, bitterness and selfishness. This can cause an "epidemic" in the church, and it could reach the incurable stage.

VI. *THE SPIRITUAL LIFE IS A LIFE OF CONSTANT GROWTH INTO CHRISTLIKENESS.*

A. 2 Cor. 3:18: "But we all, with open face beholding as in a glass the glory of the Lord, *are changed into the same image from glory to glory,* even as by the Spirit of the Lord."

It is the transformation from the self-life to Christ-likeness . . . from glory to glory. Gal. 2:20.

B. The spiritual man is ever reaching out for anything or everything spiritual. He has no appetite for the carnal. His heart "pants after God" and spiritual things as the hart after the water brooks. Psa. 42:1.

C. *The spiritual life is a life of progress.*
John 15:5: "He that abideth in me, and I in him, the same bringeth forth much fruit." Not just fruit, or more fruit, but "MUCH FRUIT." Only one branch satisfies the heart of the divine husbandman.

D. *The Father is glorified by our fruitfulness.*
John 15:8: "Herein is my Father glorified, that ye bear much fruit; so shall ye be my disciples."

131

Gal. 5:22: "But the fruit of the Spirit. . . ."

"Fruit" not fruits . . . one big cluster. All nine graces are essential to reveal Christ's beauty.

CONCLUSION: We need the gifts of the spirit, but we must first have the fruit of the spirit. A heart of love can be spoiled by a quick temper, longsuffering by boastfulness and great faith can be nulified by little gentleness. A powerful thunder of Sinai can hide the love of calvary. The embodiment of goodness can be overshadowed by worry, fretting. The spiritual life is all nine graces blending together for Him.

The Compassionate Christ

Matt. 20:29-34

INTRODUCTION: Here are two blind men, who no doubt, had tried many ways and means to receive their sight. They finally met the "all sufficient One, the CHRIST, the God-man, the Saviour. The One who went about doing good, saving the lost, healing the sick, casting out devils and relieving the oppressed. Yes, they met the WONDERFUL CHRIST. Let us notice first that:

I. JESUS PASSED THEIR WAY.

A. The blind men heard that Jesus passed by. How did they hear? Someone's testimony or maybe the voice of the multitude? They perhaps heard the multitude following Jesus. They felt the thrill of happy worshipers. All that follow Him are happy. There are no long faces, sour unhappy people following Him. ". . . happy is that people . . . whose God is the Lord." Psa. 144:15.

B. Their faith was inspired by what they heard. Rom. 10:17: "So then faith cometh by hearing, and hearing by the word of God."

C. He is passing your way today my friend, and it might be His last trip.

II. THEIR CRIES STOPPED HIM!

A. They cried out, "Have mercy on us, O Lord, thou son of David." *THE MULTITUDES REBUKED THEM*. They said the blind men should hold their peace, or in other words, "Be quiet! Don't make any noise!" or "don't get emotionally upset." This was an obstacle in their way. BUT, "They cried the more."

133

B. On one occasion Jesus was asked to make His disciples be quiet. His answer, if they ". . . hold their peace, the stones would . . . cry out." Luke 19:40. Something will always be in your way if you want to come to Jesus.

C. The very folks that yell, shout and act hysterical at some ball game or prize fight, go to church and act like a dummy or a mummy all through the service. Yet they will severely criticize those who cry out or rejoice in the Lord.

D. These men sought Jesus, not the crowd. "Seek ye the Lord while he may be found, call. . . ." Isa. 55:6. ". . . whosoever shall call. . . ." Rom. 10:13. Jesus Christ hears earnest prayer. *CRY UNTO HIM TODAY!*

III. HE ANSWERED THEIR CRY!

A. The wonderful thing about this story is, *"And Jesus stood still. . . ."* V. 32. He called them and said, "What will ye that I shall do unto you?"

B. Divinity stops for frail humanity. The infinite stands still for the finite. The heavenly king stops for earthly paupers. The Son of God stops for the sons of men.

C. Such condescension is too marvelous to comprehend. 1 Pet. 3:12: "For the eyes of the Lord are over the righteous, and his ears are open unto their prayers." Psa. 34:4: "I sought the Lord, and he heard me, and delivered me. . . ." Their need was, "Lord, that our eyes may be opened."

D. Cry unto Him today, "Lord, open my eyes." Many need to see His "all-sufficient power" to save, to sanctify, to baptize with the Holy Ghost and to heal our sick bodies. "Jesus Christ the same yesterday, and to day, and for ever." Heb. 13:8.

IV. HE HAD COMPASSION ON THEM!

A. What wonderful words! "Jesus had compassion on them, and touched their eyes: and immediately their eyes received sight." V. 34.

B. The love and compassion of the wonderful Saviour went into action. He touched them.

C. He loves us and He will touch us. He has neither lost His compassion nor His power.

V. HE MET THEIR NEED COMPLETELY.

A. They received their sight. "They followed Him." He met their need physically and spiritually.

B. The proof was "they followed Him."

CONCLUSION: If we need healing, He is the great physician. If we need salvation, He is the wonderful Saviour. If we need sanctification, He is the sanctifier. Heb. 2:11. If we need the Holy Ghost, He is the Baptizer of the Holy Ghost. Matt. 3:11. Whatever your need, "[HE] IS ABLE. . ." Eph. 3:20.

Living in the Spirit

Gal. 5:25

INTRODUCTION: Our experience with the Lord should be as the cloud and fire to the Israelites; an ever-present, over-shadowing influence. There are certain privileges and blessings that belong only to those who live in the Spirit.

I. GOD MUST BE WORSHIPED IN THE SPIRIT. John 4:23, 24

  A. Jesus told the woman at the well: "God is a Spirit: and they that worship him must worship him in spirit and in truth."

  B. The only way to worship God in spirit and truth is to be in the Spirit.

  C. The Revised Version states, "Who worship in the Spirit of God." It is not a matter of position, place or posture, but in the spirit. We may be pious, solemn and serious in our worship, but all useless unless it is in the spirit.

II. GOD'S VOICE HEARD AND GLORY WITNESSED.

  A. In Revelation 1:10, John said, "I was in the Spirit . . . and heard . . . a great voice" and saw the Son of man clothed in glory.

  B. He saw Him in His glory . . . those who live in the spirit will continually be enraptured by the glory of God.

III. HEAVENLY AND FUTURE THINGS UNDERSTOOD.

  A. Revelation 4:1, 2: "Come up hither, and I will shew thee things which must be hereafter. And immediately I was in the spirit."

136

B. Must be in the spirit to understand spiritual things. Several times John says in Revelation, "I was in the spirit."

C. The reason things to come are so little understood is because people don't live in the spirit.

D. Paul caught up in the third heaven and heard unspeakable words that were unlawful for a man to utter. 2 Cor. 12:2-5. Those in the spirit hear things the ordinary Christian never hears.

IV. GOD'S POWER SEEN WHILE IN THE SPIRIT.

A. The Lord carried me in the spirit, and set me in a valley of bones. Ezek. 37:1-10. He prophesies and life came back and they stood up. Ezekiel's message had effect.

B. Those in the spirit see God work when others cannot. They can see and feel God's mighty breath.

V. DIVINE STRENGTH AND COMFORT ARE ENJOYED BY THOSE WHO ARE IN THE SPIRIT.

A. Acts 20:22-24: ". . . behold, I go bound in the spirit . . . bonds and afflictions abide me. But none of these things move me. . . ."

B. Men in the spirit have a calm and peaceful assurance even under trying circumstances.

C. "God is our refuge. . . . [we] will not . . . fear, though the earth be removed." Psa. 46:1, 2.

VI. PROOF OF HIS DWELLING IN US.

A. Romans 8:9: ". . . in the Spirit, if so be that the Spirit of God dwell in you."

B. If He does not dwell in you, you cannot live in the spirit. Easy to talk it, but the doing is what is needed.

C. "Know ye not that ye are the temple of God, and that the Spirit of God dwelleth in you?" 1 Cor. 3:16.

D. The Spirit does not come to dwell like a candle under a bushel, or as a helpless invalid whose presence cannot be felt or seen on the outside. But as a mighty life-giving and spiritual wonder worker whose presence cannot be hid.

VII. THOSE IN THE SPIRIT CAN RENDER BETTER SERVICE TO THE MASTER.

A. Acts 6:3: ". . . look ye out among you seven men of honest report, full of the Holy Ghost and wisdom." In the Spirit and full of the Spirit is the only kind of person God can use.

B. Preaching in the Spirit. 1 Cor. 2:4: "And my speech and my preaching was not with enticing words of man's wisdom, but in demonstration of the Spirit and of power."

C. Teaching in the Spirit. Acts 18:25: Apollos taught "being fervent in the spirit."

D. Singing in the Spirit. 1 Cor. 14:15. ". . . in psalms and hymns and spiritual songs, singing and making melody in your heart to the Lord." Eph. 5:19.

E. Praying in the Spirit. Eph. 6:18: "Praying always with all prayer and supplication in the Spirit." Jude 20: ". . . praying in the Holy Ghost."

F. Romans 8:26: "Likewise the Spirit also helpeth our infirmities: for we know not what we should pray for as we ought: but the Spirit itself maketh intercession for us with groanings which cannot be uttered."

CONCLUSION: Gal. 5:16: "Walk in the Spirit, and ye shall not fulfil the lust of the flesh." The church would run good if we kept ourselves full of the oil of the Spirit.

Dilemma and Deliverance

"I said, Lord, be merciful unto me: heal my soul; for I have sinned against thee." Psa. 41:4.

INTRODUCTION: This was probably stated after he had committed his great sin, the sin of adultery and murder. When Nathan, the prophet, confronted him, he said, "I have sinned." In Psa. 51:1, 2, he cried out, ". . . blot out my transgressions. Wash me throughly from mine iniquity, and cleanse me from my sin."

David took the position every backslider and sinner must take, penitent, patient and prisoner.

I. FIRST, THE PENITENT.

A. I have sinned against thee. Be merciful unto me. "Against thee, thee only, have I sinned. . . ." Psa. 51:4.

B. Achan: "I have sinned." Josh. 7:20.
Judas: "I have sinned." Matt. 27:4.
Saul: "I have sinned." 1 Sam. 15:24.
Prodigal: "I have sinned." Luke 15:18.

C. Some say, "All I do is against myself. . . .I don't harm anybody nor is it against God." But this is not the truth. Every sin is a personal insult to our most high God, and calls for a contrite confession.

D. It is a clenched fist upraised in the face of God —defying God. It is the bitter answer of earth's hate to heaven's eternal love.

E. God says in 1 John 3:4, "Quit sinning, you are transgressing my law." Sin is a transgressor of the law. God says, "Come . . . let us reason together." Isa. 1:18. The sinner who continues in sin shouts, "NO!" in the face of God.

139

F. Since every sin is a violation of divine law and in defiance of the divine authority, it must be repented of and confessed.

G. John the Baptist, preached repentance. Matt. 3:2. Jesus preached it. Luke 13:3, 5. Peter, "Repent ye therefore, and be converted. . . ." Acts 3:19. Paul ". . . commandeth all men every where to repent." Acts 17:30.

H. The sinner is guilty of breaking God's law and is a convicted rebel. Therefore, he should repent and cry, "Be merciful unto me."

II. SECOND, A PATIENT.

A. He was willing to enter into heaven's hospital as a patient. David prayed, "Heal my soul." He wanted spiritual treatment. He cried out, "HEAL MY SOUL."

B. There is much said about healing of the body, but the healing most needed is "SOUL" healing. When we pray God heal my body, we admit something has gone wrong with it. It is either diseased or afflicted.

C. Sin will disease, afflict and ruin the soul. "Every sin" is a self-inflicted gash or wound on the sinner's soul.

D. Habakkuk 2:10: "Thou . . . hast sinned against thy soul." Job 24:12: ". . . the soul of the wounded crieth out." Psa. 33:19: ". . . deliver their soul from death."

E. Sin in the soul is incurable by any earthly means. Isa. 55:3: ". . . come unto me: hear, and your soul shall live."

F. A repentant sinner can leave out of the heavenly hospital a spiritually well man. Isa. 55:2: ". . . let your soul delight itself in fatness."

140

G. Many need this operation. Healed by the Great Physician. No man with cancer, tuberculosis, or leprosy can be fully happy.

H. Wounded souls are not happy, but thank God, Jesus is "the great physician" and He can restore to health and happiness.

Psa. 23:3: "He restoreth my soul."

Psa. 51:12: "Restore unto me the joy of thy salvation."

In the place of a diseased and downcast soul, you can have a healthy and happy soul. Why be bound by the cancer of sin any longer? "If the Son therefore shall make you free, ye shall be free indeed." John 8:36.

III. THIRD, A PRISONER.

A. He cried out, "Lord, be merciful unto me." The sinner is before the heavenly tribunal—guilty and condemned.

B. He is before the Judge of all the earth. Gen. 19:25. He is at the bench, the bar of justice to receive sentence.

C. John 3:18: ". . . he that believeth not is condemned already."

D. But there must be witnesses to his guilt. The following give their testimonies:

1. *The Law says,* he has sinned, and has broken the law of God. 1 John 3:4. "For whosoever shall keep the whole law, and yet offend in one point, he is guilty of all." James 2:10.

2. *Conscience*—His conscience is smitten, condemned, haunting his soul. It testifies against him.

3. *Society says,* Yes, he is a sinner. Drunkard, gambler, curser, outcast, etc.

141

4. *His neighbors*—"I have seen his sin." He is mean and vile and there is nothing good in him.

5. *His relatives say,* "Sure he is a sinner. He never prayed or lived for God."

6. *The devil who is called our adversary accuses him.* 1 Peter 5:8.

E. *The verdict:* The answer must be, *"YOU ARE GUILTY."*

F. But the "You are guilty" turns to "YOU ARE FORGIVEN" when you confess your sins and believe Him for salvation. God says because you have repented and confessed, if you will accept My forgiveness, My healing and pardon, you may go in peace.

CONCLUSION: Jesus will forgive, heal and pardon to-day. Rev. 3:20. John 7:37: "If any man thirst, let him come unto me, and drink." All that come to Him, good or bad, will be forgiven. Rev. 22:17.

Harvesttime

Matt. 9:36-38

INTRODUCTION: Jesus saw the multitude as sheep without a shepherd. He had compassion on them. He likened the great crowd to a harvest. This text suggests an abundant harvest.

I. PLENTY WORK TO BE DONE

A. "The harvest truly is plenteous." V. 37.

B. It is an enormous task. It is a great field. Jesus said, "The field is the world." Matt. 13:88.

C. There are many nations of the world, but only half have heard the real gospel. The large field does not frighten us, but the next suggestion does.

II. SCARCITY OF WORKERS

A. ". . . the labourers are few." V. 37. Laborers? Not fortune hunters . . . not fame followers . . . nor position parasites . . . nor glory grabbers . . . but laborers. It is work, hard work. "He that goeth forth and weepeth. . . . Psa. 126:6.

B. It is a very plenteous harvest and the harvest is ripe. An abundance of loafers, but few laborers. What a pity! Most of professed Christians turn deaf ears to the Master's voice. No matter how loud the Macedonian cry, many refuse to respond.

III. PRAYER IS NECESSARY TO SUCCESSFUL WORK OF CHRISTIANS

A. "Pray ye therefore the Lord of the harvest. . . ." V. 38.

143

B. 2 Chron. 7:14: "If my people, which are called by my name, shall humble themselves, and pray . . . then. . . ."

C. *Two reasons why we are asked to pray.*

1. Because many need to be moved or impelled to go. Some render this scripture, "that he will send forth [thrust forth]" (v. 38), to intimates an UNWILLINGNESS TO GO. This is probably because of weakness and being afraid of hardships and opposition. So, we ought to pray. We are commanded to pray.

2. Because if God does not send some forth, others will go simply because of sympathy. And some will go because they believe there is adventure and glamor in gospel work.

IV. LABORERS MUST BE GOD-SENT

A. Because He is "the Lord of the harvest." V. 38. ". . . my father is the husbandman." John 15:1. He is Master and Lord of the harvest.

B. He understands and knows how it should be harvested and when, therefore He knows exactly who would be best to go.

C. "As thou hast sent me into the world, even so have I also sent them. . . ." John 17:18.

D. "There was a man sent from God. . . ." John 1:6.

E. Paul and Barnabas, "Being sent forth by the Holy Ghost." Acts 13:1-4.

V. DANGER OF LOSING THE BURDEN AND PASSION FOR SOULS

A. ". . . he that sleepeth in harvest. . . ." Prov. 10:5. He is not condemning sleep, BUT because of sleeping while there is work to be done. This shows unconcerness, complacency. "Woe to them that are at ease in Zion." Amos 6:1.

B. *People must sleep . . . But not on the job.* Examples: Nurse; surgeon; policeman; fireman; engineer; soldier; signalman in railroad tower; lighthouse keeper; and gospel preacher.

C. Robert Browning said, "Be sure they sleep not, whom God needs."

D. A sleeping man is a useless man. NO USE TO MAKE AN IMPASSIONED APPEAL TO HIM ABOUT GOD'S HARVEST FIELD, FOR HE IS ASLEEP. He is deaf to all holier calls. He is blind to all the loftier visions. He is a spiritual nonentity. He DOES NOT COUNT.

He weighs nothing on God's scale of requirements. He is as powerless as a tombstone. THE CHURCH NEEDS HIM. GOD NEEDS HIM. LOST SOULS NEED HIM. BUT, HE IS ASLEEP. . . . Selected.

VI. THE URGENCY IS UNMISTAKABLE

Jesus told His disciples to ". . . Lift up your eyes, and look on the fields; for they are white already to harvest." John 4:35.

The Task Is Urgent, Because:

A. *The harvest will not wait.* Harvesttime is crisis time. Ripened grain must be gathered or be lost. Doors once opened and unentered may close again. We must strike while the iron is hot. It is now or never.

B. *The harvest will not reap itself.* The harvest needs men to reap it, and women to glean in the corners, like Ruth. Unless men and women see the vision of whitened fields, the golden

145

grain will be lost. No one can do your job. What you fail to reap will be lost.

C. *Harvesttime is a busy time.* It is no time to play . . . no time to sleep. All hands must be at work. There must be no loafers . . . no sluggards . . . no drones. It is time to labor . . . time to work.

VII. THE REWARD FOR OUR LABOR IS CERTAIN

A. "They that sow in tears shall reap in joy. He that goeth forth and weepeth, bearing precious seed, shall doubtless come again with rejoicing." Psa. 126:5, 6.

B. ". . . weeping may endure for a night, but joy cometh in the morning." Psa. 30:5.

C. *What a glorious promise!* Doubtless come again . . . without doubt. And come with rejoicing. Rejoicing because of sheaves to lay at the Master's feet.

CONCLUSION: Are we saying as the disciples, "Four months and then the harvest." Or as Christ, "White already to harvest."

Let us throw our all into the winning of souls in this crucial hour. Is the harvest song in our hearts? Is the harvest blade in our hands?

BE SURE THEY SLEEP NOT WHOM GOD NEEDS. HE THAT SLEEPETH IN TIME OF HARVEST IS A SON THAT CAUSETH SHAME. Prov. 10:5.

Determined to Die

Isa. 50:7; Luke 22:22

INTRODUCTION: Even from the time He left His heavenly home, Christ was headed for the cross. This had been decided in the courts of heaven by the Great Triune Godhead. It was the only way to effect reconciliation between God and man. During His earthly ministry, His betrayal, His trial and crucifixion, there were appeals for Him to take the easy road and bypass the way of the cross. He resisted them all.

I. PETER, (A FRIEND) UNKNOWINGLY SUGGESTED IT.

   A. "Be it far from thee, Lord: this shall not be unto thee." Matt. 16:21-23. This statement was made because Christ said that He must "suffer many things . . . and be killed. . . ." V. 21.

      Even though it was an impulsive statement, it was said out of love for Christ.

   B. Peter felt that One so great should not have to suffer and die.

   C. It was stated from a protective standpoint.

   D. Friends with good intentions can hinder us from obeying God's will.

II. THE FLESH APPEALED FOR AN EASIER WAY.

      of suffering. It is opposed to the law of God and the Spirit of God. Rom. 8:5-8. This was evidenced by Christ's prayer in the garden, ". . . if it be possible, let this cup pass from me." Matt. 26:39.

147

". . . the spirit . . . is willing, but the flesh is weak." Matt. 26:41.

B. It is true that He was God "manifest in the flesh." 1 Tim. 3:16. But it is also true that He was "the man Christ Jesus." 1 Tim. 2:5. He frequently called Himself "the Son of man." He was "in all points tempted like as we are. . . ." Heb. 4:15.

C. But, He conquered the flesh. The Scripture says, "he . . . suffered in the flesh." 1 Pet. 4:1. He had to battle against fleshly feelings and desires like any other man. But, thank God, He was always the overcomer.

D. We must follow the example of our Lord, "who walk not after the flesh." Rom. 8:4. For "they that are in the flesh cannot please God." Rom. 8:8. "For if ye live after the flesh, ye shall die. . . ." Rom. 8:13.

III. SATAN, (THE ENEMY OF ALL RIGHTEOUS-NESS) OFFERED HIM AN EASIER WAY. Matt. 4:8, 9.

A. The enemy, Satan, the devil, made a desperate move to detour Christ from the cross. He showed Jesus "all the kingdoms of the world, and the glory of them; And said unto him, All these things will I give thee if thou wilt fall down and worship me."

B. Someone has said, "They were not his to give." But, Jesus did not question his right to make the offer. In a certain sense, He probably could have done it. Of course, not in the absolute sense.

C. Jesus rejected Satan's offer by saying, "Get thee hence, Satan: for it is written, Thou shalt worship the Lord thy God, and. . . ."

D. Christ knew His death on the cross would re-

148

deem mankind, and that He would in God's time be "King of kings, and Lord of lords." Rev. 19:16.

IV. THE GENERAL PUBLIC CHALLENGED HIM TO PROVE HIS DEITY.

A. Matt. 27:39, 40: "If thou be the Son of God, come down. . . ." This is the same old "IF" Satan had used before. Matt. 4:3, 6.

B. Christ would not yield to one, nor to a few, nor to a mutitude.

C. He was determined to die for the sins of the people.

D. Uncommitted people yield to the pressure of circumstances and personalities.

V. THE CHIEF PRIESTS, SCRIBES AND ELDERS (RELIGIOUS LEADERS) WERE USED OF SATAN TO TEMPT HIM TO COME DOWN. Matt. 27:41, 42.

A. They mocked Him.

B. They said, "He saved others; himself he cannot save."

C. "If he be the King of Israel, let him now come down from the cross, and we will believe him."

D. Abraham said to the rich man, they will not "be persuaded, though one rose from the dead." Luke 16:31.

VI. THE THIEVES ALSO "CAST THE SAME IN HIS TEETH." Matt. 27:44.

A. "He trusted in God; let him deliver him now. . . ." V. 43. And they said, "Thou that destroyest the temple, and buildest it in three days, save thyself. If thou be the Son of God, come down from the cross. V. 40.

149

B. Luke 23:39: ". . . one of the malefactors . . . railed on him, saying, If thou be Christ, save thyself and us."

C. They tried to get Christ to prove publicly that God, the Father, loved Him and would deliver Him from the cross.

D. Christ did not need this assurance.

E. And, He knew it would not change the opinions of the thieves or the others.

VI. THE SOLDIERS JOINED OTHERS IN TAUNTING HIM. Mark 15:16-20.

A. They "mocked him."

B. ". . . they smote him on the head . . . spit upon him," and mockingly "bowing their knees worshipped him."

C. They offered Him vinegar.

D. "If thou be the king of the Jews, save thyself." Luke 23:36, 37. They tempted Jesus to prove His power and kingship.

E. He was on His way to the throne, but they didn't know it.

VIII. BUT THE THREE MARYS STOOD BY HIS CROSS IN SILENT SUBMISSION.

A. "Now there stood by the cross of Jesus his mother, and his mother's sister, Mary the wife of Cleophas, and Mary Magdalene." John 19:25.

B. They had "ministered unto him. . . ." Mark 15: 41. They seemed to have a deeper discernment than the others. "And many women . . . ministering unto him." Matt. 27:55.

C. And, perhaps they had reached the conclusion

that Christ must die to save the people from their sins.

IX. HE HAD THREE AVENUES OF ESCAPE.

A. *Using diplomacy on Pilate,* (1) He could have negotiated peace terms. (2) He could have arranged a compromise.

B. *Appealing to the multitude.* He could have appealed unto them on the basis that He had healed many of them. He had cleansed the lepers, made the lame to walk, the blind to see, the deaf to hear, and those bound were set free.

C. *Using His supernatural power.* He could have called "twelve legions of angels" to release Him. Matt. 26:53.

X. HE CHOSE THE PREDETERMINED AND PROPHESIED WAY . . . THE WAY OF THE CROSS.

A. "And truly the Son of man goeth, as it was determined: but woe unto that man by whom he is betrayed!" Luke 22:22.

B. "Then said I, Lo, I come (in the volume of the book it is written of me,) to do thy will, O God." Heb. 10:7. (See Psa. 40:7, 8.) ". . . nevertheless not my will, but thine, be done." Luke 22: 42.

C. The prophets told of His ill-treatment and the death He was to die for the salvation of mankind. Isa. 53:1-11; Psa. 22:12-18.

CONCLUSION: He set His "face like a flint." Isa. 50: 6, 7. He was determined to die. He gave Himself for us, the just for the unjust. He died that we might live.

The Lack of Faith

Mark 4:40

INTRODUCTION: Someone said, "Faith is in the church." This is true, however, no one will deny that the church needs more faith. The lack of proper food causes certain conditions in the body. A lack of faith also causes certain conditions in the spiritual man. 2 Cor. 5:7: "We walk by faith, not by sight." The more faith, the straighter we walk. The Word of God declares that "The just shall live by faith," Rom. 1:17. Goethe, the German poet said, "If you have any faith, give me, for heaven's sake, a share of it! Your doubts you may keep to yourself for I have plenty of my own."

I. THE LACK OF FAITH PRODUCES "FEAR."

A. *"Why are ye so fearful?* how is it . . . ye have no faith?" Mark 4:40. If we don't have faith, we have something else, unbelief. Jesus didn't say, "How is it you have no "courage?" But He said, "How is it you have no 'faith'?" He strikes at the root of the trouble—unbelief.

B. *"Fear hath torment"* 1 John 4:18. It is one of Satan's most effective weapons. Fear of death— fear of man—fear of suffering—fear of falling— all are fruits of unbelief.

C. *Perfect love casteth out fear.* Faith brings in love. George McDonald said, "A perfect faith would lift us absolutely above fear." We are powerless to deal with this inward fear. The root and source must be dealt with. We must seek God until love and faith floods our souls, then fear and doubts will vanish. Someone has said, "feed your faith and your doubts will starve to death."

D. *Faith and fear cannot live in the same house.*

152

No house is large enough for two families. Our lives are controlled by one or the other. Matt. 6:24. It has been well said, "He who has lost confidence can lose nothing more."

II. THE LACK OF FAITH CAUSES "REASONINGS."

A. *"O ye of little faith, why reason ye among yourselves."* Reasonings of a carnal mind is destructive to real faith. Christ told them to beware of the leaven of the Pharisees. He meant doctrine, principles, practices, the souring, spreading, swelling of false religion. They thought He was speaking of bread.

B. When they reasoned, He said, "How little trust you have in me." Moffatt.
Human reasoning reaches no higher than meat and bread; the temporal.
He reminds them that He has always supplied bread.

C. We should not reason in our hearts, will Christ do this? Can He do that? But remind ourselves that He has already done it. Jesus did not say, "O ye of little sense" or "O ye of little ability." It is not lack of sense or a lack of ability, but lack of faith that caused trouble.

D. John Fletcher said, "You must shut the eye of carnal reason and stop the ear of the reasonings of the serpent, which were your's to listen to him, would be endless and would soon draw you out of your way of faith."

E. Jesus definitely attributes these unspiritual reasonings to unbelief. Open the eye of faith and see the faithfulness of God and His Word. The devil says, "You can't make it." God's Word says, "he is able to keep that which I have committed unto him. . . ." 2 Tim. 1:12.

153

III. THE LACK OF FAITH DEFEATS THE PURPOSE OF GOD.

A. Matt. 13:58: *"And he did not many mighty works there because of their unbelief."*
Moffatt, v. 58: "There he could not do many miracles owing to their lack of faith."

B. God's works of grace are largely, if not altogether, conditional on faith. John Wesley said, "God does nothing except in answer to 'believing' prayer."

C. Mark 6:5, 6: "And he could there do no mighty work, save that he laid his hands upon a few sick folk, and healed them. And he marvelled because of their unbelief." Moffatt, v. 6: "He was astonished at their lack of faith."

D. He couldn't do His mighty works because of a wall of unbelief. His hands were stopped; His ministry curtailed; or limited, because of the lack of faith. Oh! How we need to awake to His love and power, to wait in eager expectation for miraculous workings in our midst.

E. God is good—expect then to see it manifested. God is love—rejoice then, continually in Him. God is almighty—be surprised at nothing He can and will do.
God is faithful—depend on Him to fulfill His promises.

F. Unbelief, or lack of faith is that hurtful, harmful, hindering, halting and hell-inspired element that is choking life out of churches and individual saints today.

IV. THE LACK OF FAITH PUTS A VEIL UPON OUR HEARTS.

A. 2 Cor. 3:15: "But even unto this day, when Moses is read, the vail is upon their heart."

This, of course, is speaking about the Jews. (v. 14). "But their minds were blinded: for until this day remaineth the same vail untaken away in the reading of the old testament." Unbelief "blinded their minds."

B. Rom. 11:20: ". . . because of unbelief they were broken off, and thou standest by faith."
When they could see, they wouldn't, now, they cannot. The veil is upon their heart. They are blind.

C. Rom. 11:21: "For if God spared not the natural branches, take heed lest he also spare not thee." The soul, like the body, has various senses whereby it apprehends the spiritual blessings of God.

D. The Word of God speaks of seeing, hearing, feeling, tasting. Unbelief, (evil principles within) puts a veil upon our hearts and dulls our spiritual sensibilities. It paralizes our power of appropriating deep and spiritual blessings for our souls.

E. But by waiting upon God in humility and faith, we can "taste" and see that God is good.
Hear—the voice in the burning bush.
See—God in nature, in His people, His Word.
Feel—His loving presence with us.
Smell—His garments of myrrh, aloes and cassia.
The veil is gone. We can believe fully.

F. Who has the veil today? Those who receive not the "love of the truth. . . . God shall send them strong delusion. . . . believed not the truth. . . ." 2 Thess. 2:10-12.

V. THE LACK OF FAITH ROBS US OF POWER.

A. The disciples asked, "Why could not we cast him out?" Matt. 17:19, 20. Jesus said, *"Because of your unbelief."*

155

Moffatt, "Your faith is so little."

B. Unbelief not only robs us of spiritual joy and acts as a veil on our hearts, but robs us of power with God and man. God wants us to have power with Him. Peter said, ". . . such as I have give . . . rise up and walk." Acts 3:6.

C. Luke 10:19: "I give unto you power. . . ." Acts 1:8: "Ye shall receive power. . . ."

VI. THE LACK OF FAITH CAUSES US TO DEPART FROM GOD.

A. Heb. 3:12: "Take heed, brethren, lest there be in any of you an evil heart of unbelief, in departing from the living God."

Here is the crux, the climax of the whole matter, an "evil heart of unbelief." Others are outposts—this is the stronghold.

B. There are two things about this inward enemy we should consider.

1. *The lack of faith is something the heart is unconscious of until revealed by the Holy Ghost.* The most searching analysis cannot find it. Pride, vanity, self-love, jealously, etc. are the firstfruits of it, but INWARD UNBELIEF, THE HOLY GHOST MUST FIND IT. We must humble our soul before Him if we want to be rid of it.

2. *The lack of faith is deeper than our wills.* When we really want to serve God, but somehow we are always losing ground, missing the mark, failing God, departing from Him, we need to seek God until the Holy Ghost reveals the inward sin. David cried, "Search me . . . And see if there be any wicked way in me." Psalm 139:23, 24.

C. The devil has injected the poison of unbelief into

the very nature of man—into the blood streams, until it has become a part of him. It seems natural to doubt God and His promises, to have delusions of false doctrines, to believe the devil and backslide because of worldly pursuits.

D. The cause will be unrecognized, unacknowledged, unsuspected and unconfessed. But, the "evil heart of unbelief" will remain. Oh! That we might detect it, confess it, and cast it out forever.

VII. IT BRINGS CONDEMNATION.

A. John 3:18: ". . . *he that believeth not is condemned already,* because he hath not believed. . . ."

B. "Whatsoever is not of faith is sin." Rom. 14:23.

C. Jesus said to His disciples, "Where is your faith?" Luke 8:25.

CONCLUSION: "Lord, I believe; help thou mine unbelief." Mark 9:24.

Jesus, Our Example in Prayer

Luke 11:1

INTRODUCTION: It is not to be supposed that His disciples had never prayed, but something they saw and heard in His prayer made them want to pray. They had heard Him (1) preach, but never asked Him to teach them to preach; they had seen Him (2) cast out devils, but never asked to be taught to cast out devils; they had seen Him (3) heal the sick, but didn't ask Him to teach them to heal. They had seen His (4) power over the elements, but never asked for this kind of power. But they did request Him, "Lord teach us to pray."

(1) He gives them a pattern for prayer, vv. 2-4. (2) He urges persistence in prayer, vv. 5-8. (3) He emphasizes possibilities in prayer, vv. 9-13.

I. PRAYER WAS THE HABITUAL ATMOSPHERE OF HIS DAILY LIFE.

A. This can be found on many pages of the Gospels. We see Him *rising up in the early morning* to pray. Mark 1:35: "And in the morning, rising up a great while before day, he went out, and departed into a solitary place, and there prayed." *While others slept, He prayed.*

B. *After a day of hard work while others rest . . .* He prays. "And when he had sent them away, he departed into a mountain to pray." Mark 6:46.

C. *When crowds surged upon Him,* invaded His privacy and clamored greedily for His help, "And looking up to heaven, he sighed, and saith unto him, Ephphatha, that is, Be opened." Mark 7:34.

D. Not only was it an important part of His life . . . it was HIS LIFE . . . THE VERY BREATH OF HIS BEING. This means that things which

158

commonly hinder and stifle our prayer life, had no power at all with Him.

II. HIS PRAYER LIFE WAS NEVER AT THE MERCY OF MOODS.

A. *Changes of feeling* He certainly knew, but this caused no change in His praying. *He knew joy, sorrow, smiles,* tears and weariness, but through it all His heart turned to prayer.

B. Like a compass, His heart turned to His Father. He loved Him and could not bear to be away from Him. He used every opportunity, day and night, to speak to the One He loved best.

C. *When we fail in praying,* because of our *moods* (our feelings) it is *a symptom of something deeper, a breakdown of our affection.* It shows lack of love for God.

III. HE WOULD NOT ALLOW BUSYNESS TO STIFLE HIS PRAYER LIFE.

A. *There are hinderances to prayer.* The days become so full, prayer is crowded out. Jesus never allowed this in His work for His Heavenly Father.

B. *The opening chapters of Mark's Gospel* shows His busy days—Many pressing on Him—Clamoring for His services, far into the night. Yet, *the harder His days, the more He prayed.*

C. *The World's greatest toiler* was the greatest shining example of the daily, hourly practice of the presence of God. He condoned no substitute for prayer.

D. No matter how busy a man's life is there can be —there must be—time for prayer. "And when he had sent the multitudes away, he went up into a mountain apart to pray: and when the evening was come, he was there alone." Matt. 14:23.

159

IV. HE DID NOT ALLOW IMPATIENCE TO HINDER THE SERIOUS BUSINESS OF PRAYER.

A. Most of us knock once, if the door opens—wonderful! If not, we turn away impatiently—we cannot wait. How different with Him!

B. The writer of Hebrews speaks of Jesus offering up "prayers and supplications with strong crying and tears unto him that was able to save him. . . ." Heb. 5:7. Whatever else this may mean, it certainly means that prayer to Jesus was a serious, and strenuous business that involved every energy of mind, heart and soul.

C. The same truth shines out in Luke 11:5-10, ". . . yet because of his importunity he will rise and give him as many as he needeth." (Amplified New Testament). "Because of His *shameless persistence and insistence* he will get up and give him as much as he needs." Jesus calls him and blesses him for his shamelessness. "That is the very spirit of prayer," He says, in effect. "Take no denial! Knock again! Beat upon heaven's gates!"

D. He did not imply that God is unwilling, but what He meant to teach was that lackadaisical, half-hearted praying is worse than useless. *Many times God requires persistence as proof of earnestness before He answers prayer.*

E. EXAMPLE (1) *The Syrophenician woman.* Mark 7: 25-30. (2) *The widow and the unjust judge.* Luke 18:1-8. "This widow is such a great nuisance that I will see her righted before she wears me out with her persistence." Luke 18:5— Phillips Translation, ". . . lest she give me intolerable annoyance and wear me out by her continual coming, or lest she come and rail on me, or assault me or strangle me." (3) *Blind Bar-*

160

timaeus. Mark 10:46. No threats could silence him. (4) *The four faithful* found the door closed and raised the roof. Mark 2:4. (5) *Elijah prayed* seven times. (6) *Jacob prayed* all night. (7) *Daniel prayed* 21 days.

F. Impatience in prayer stands rebuked by the prayer life of Jesus and others who prevailed in prayer.

V. DIFFERENT ELEMENTS IN OUR LORD'S PRAYER. (Communion, thanksgiving, petition, intercession).

A. *Communion. An Element in His Prayer.* Often He would turn to God . . . not for a gift . . . but for fellowship. "as he prayed, the fashion of his countenance was altered." Luke 9:29.

1. This is the prayer of communion, when heart speaks to heart—the utter intimacy of prayer that brings the glow. Communion shows we are not serving God for conveniences but for love.

2. No lasting human friendship could be based on mere matters of convenience—always approaching friend for favors and at no other time—our friendship would be questioned. No friendship could survive on such a basis.

3. Jesus would have us go to God when there is nothing to ask, go to Him not for gifts but for Himself alone. That is the prayer of communion—when a loving heart goes out Godward in this way, God comes to meet it, and the heart experiences the *Blessed Invasion of God's Presence.*

B. *Thanksgiving, Another Element in His Prayer.*

1. It was often praise and thanksgiving that drove Him to His knees, not only in sunshine, but

161

in hours of darkness, His gratitude was un-
quenched. He took the broken bread, symbol
of His broken body, and gave God thanks.
Luke 22:19. He went out of the Upper Room
to the sweat and agony of Gethsemane. He
sings a hymn of praise—Mark 14:26.

C. *The Next Element Is Petition.*

1. We have already seen that petition is not the
   only reason for approaching God. But it certainly is a reason.

2. Prevailing opinion in modernist circles that
   prayer of petition is childish and should have
   no place in the life of a well-developed and
   mature Christian, is theory and entirely false,
   for Jesus never outgrew it.

3. He settles this forever by teaching His disciples
   to say, "Our Father." If He is really *Our Father*
   and we *His Children,* then it would be un-
   natural not to being our petitions to Him.
   Such petition should be subject to "Thy Will
   be done" for at times God's wisdom may have
   to refuse what our heart craves.

4. He taught us to ask. Matt. 7:7, 8; John 14:14;
   John 15:7; Matt. 21:22.

D. *The Final Element Was Intercession.*

1. *He prayed for His enemies.* Luke 23:34, "Father, forgive. . . ."

2. *He prayed for His disciples.* John 17:9, "I
   pray for them: I pray not for the world. . . ."

3. *He prayed for Peter.* Luke 22:31, 32. "I have
   prayed for thee, that thy faith fail not."

VI. HE PRAYED AT ALL GREAT CRISIS OF HIS
CAREER.

A. *He Is Here Praying About His Vocation.*

"The day" when His call came, a sudden, swift summon to His life's work, "It came to pass," says Luke, "that Jesus also being baptized, and praying, the heaven was opened, And the Holy Ghost descended. . . ." Luke 3:21, 22.

B. *Praying for Guidance.*

1. The Pharisees were mad at Him. They were very critical of His work. Luke 6:11: "They were filled with madness."

2. The day came when He faced the momentous decision of choosing the first Apostolic Group, And "he went out into a mountain to pray, and continued all night in prayer." Luke 6: 12.

3. The "day" when the disciples were baffled by a difficult case of demon possession and gave it up as hopeless, Jesus points them to prayer and fasting. Mark 9:29.

C. *Praying When His Popularity Was the Highest.*

Luke 5:15, 16: "But so much the more went there a fame abroad of him: and great multitudes came together to hear, and to be healed by him of their infirmities. And he withdrew himself into the wilderness, and prayed."

D. *Praying Against Temptation.*

That "day" when darkness of Gethsemane closed in on Him and the temptation to desert God's high road harrasses Him like a temptest—but *HE PRAYED.* "Being in an agony he prayed." Luke 22:44.

E. *He Died Praying.*

"Finally the day" when the nails and torture of Calvary had almost finished their work—His strength ebbing away—water of Jordan rolling at

His feet—"Father, into thy hands I commend my spirit." Luke 23:46.

CONCLUSION: In all the great crisis of His life He prayed and even in the moment of death He prayed. From the beginning of His ministry until His last breath on Calvary, He was continually praying. How can we claim to be His followers unless we do the same?

Man-Made Religion

1 Kings 12:26-33

INTRODUCTION: Jeroboam, the son of Nebat, although of the race of Joshua, became a ringleader in sin. Seeds of thought sprang up in his heart and mind and ran wild. In place of cutting out the wild weeds of godless thoughts, they grew and spread unto his downfall. He forsook the right way of the Lord and started a new religion, designed to aid his own selfish aims.

I. THIS MAN-MADE RELIGION HAD ITS ORIGIN IN THE HUMAN HEART.

"... *Jeroboam said in his heart.* ..." V. 26.

A. There are only two religions. The "I think" of man and the "I will" of God. God has said for all time, "... my thoughts are not your thoughts, neither are your ways my ways. ..." Isa. 55:8.

B. "The heart is deceitful above all things, and desperately wicked. ..." Jer. 17:9.

C. "There is a way that seemeth right unto a man, but. ..." Prov. 16:25.

D. Out of the human heart can come nothing to meet the claims of God, nor the need of the soul. Revelation from God is needed. Thank God it has been given. Anything opposed to, or used as a substitute, is gross presumption and rebellion.

II. IT WAS FOR HIS OWN SELFISH ENDS.

A. *He set up his own "golden calves"* ... one in Bethel and the other in Dan. The reason for it, he was afraid their hearts would be turned from him. It was a religion that centered on his own personal honor and welfare. It was a self-centered act.

165

B. Self is forever the center of all godless religion. Christ is the center of true religion.

C. The pride of life lies at the root of all human schemes. 1 John 2:15, 16.

D. The religion of Scribes and Pharisees was another form of the sin of Jeroboam. Rom. 10:3.

III. HE CLAIMED IT WAS FOR THE GOOD OF OTHERS.

A. Jeroboam said, *"It is too much for you to go up to Jerusalem."* He pretended it was for their convenience and advantage. Religion born of carnal hearts can only make hypocrites.

B. How could Jeroboam make this false god; dishonoring Israel? What hypocrisy! What idolatry!

C. ". . . behold thy gods, O Israel, which brought thee up out of the land of Egypt." (v. 28). Notice that self-denial was carefully excluded from all his religious arrangements.

IV. IT WAS CONTRARY TO THE WORD OF GOD.

A. *It was a lie.* Jeroboam made two calves of gold. This was an idolatrous act. The command of God was plain. (v. 28). Ex. 20:4: "Thou shalt not make unto thee any graven image."

B. Psalm 106:20: "Thus they changed their glory into the similitude of an ox that eateth grass." The carnal mind walks by sight and not by faith.

C. Naaman in his self-centeredness and self-esteem was humiliated and angered when told to "go and wash in Jordan seven times." He said, ". . . *I thought,* He will surely come out to me. . . ." 2 Kings 5:11.

D. The Apostle Paul said, *"I verily thought with myself,* that I ought to do many things contrary to the name of Jesus of Nazareth." Acts 26:9.

V. IT BECAME A SNARE TO OTHERS.

A. *The thing became a sin.* V. 30. The thing "set up" became the "object" of worship instead of a means to help people get to God. What a tragedy!

B. God is good. His way is plain, but many people all through the ages have devised and designed their own ways to their utter destruction. And much worse, they have led millions astray from the plain paths of peace and righteousness.

CONCLUSION: The thing, NO MATTER WHAT IT IS, that takes the place of God, becomes sin. Let us be watchful for the false and hold fast to the true.

A Living Refuge

Isa. 32:2

INTRODUCTION: "A man shall be as an hiding place. . . ." Not a system, church, ritual, ceremony, creed, dogma or doctrine, but A MAN. Yes, Jesus was a man. It is true that He was *very God,* but it is also true that He was *very man.* He was divine, yet He was also human. John 1:14. "The man Christ Jesus. . . ." 1 Tim. 2:5. He was sinless, yet accursed. The beloved of God, yet exposed to the wind and tempest of men and devils.

I. THIS MAN SAVES

A. *He is "an hiding place."*

B. Heb. 7:25: "Wherefore he is able also to save them to the uttermost. . . ."

C. Matt. 1:21: "And she shall bring forth a son, and . . . he shall save his people from their sins."

D. He saved a woman in adultery. John 8:11; Luke 19:5-9.

E. He saved and set free the Demoniac of Gadara. Mark 5:8-15.

F. Our refuge is a living man, with a loving, glowing, heart-throbbing compassion for the souls of men.

G. He invites all to come to Him. Matt. 11:28: "Come unto me, all ye that . . . are heavy laden, and I will give you rest." Rom. 10:13: ". . . whosoever shall call upon the name of the Lord shall be saved." Rev. 22:17: ". . . whosoever will, let him take the water of life freely."

H. He hides us from the howling winds of temptation. Col. 3:3 tells us that our "life is hid with Christ in God."

168

II. THIS MAN SATISFIES

A. He is as *"rivers of water in a dry place."*

B. These rivers of waters speak of the abounding fullness of Christ toward all those who abide in Him.

C. John 4:14: "But whosoever drinketh of the water that I shall give him *shall never thirst;* but the water that I shall give him shall be in him a well. . . ."

D. John 7:37: "In the last day, that great day of the feast, Jesus stood and cried, saying, If any man thirst, let him come unto me, and drink."

E. Psa. 103:5: *"Who satisfieth thy mouth* with good things; so that thy youth is renewed like the eagle's."

F. Jesus, in His great sermon, said, "I am the bread of life; he that cometh to me *shall never hunger;* and he that believeth on me *shall never thirst."* John 6:35.

G. ". . . in the days of famine they shall be satisfied." Psa. 37:19.

III. THIS MAN SHELTERS

A. *He is as "the shadow of a great rock in a weary land."*

B. This way at times may be weary.

1. It is weary because it is rough. Trials may come thick and fast, but He is the shadow.

2. It is weary because it is long. And suffering may make it seem longer. But we are safe when abiding in the shadow of His holy Presence.

3. It is weary because it is lonely. When it seems

we are alone, He is the cool refreshing shadow of a great rock in a weary land.

4. Psa. 91:1, 4: "He that dwelleth in the secret place of the most High shall abide under the shadow of the Almighty. . . . He shall cover thee with his feathers, and under his wings shalt thou trust. . . ."

5. Psa. 61:3: "For thou hast been a shelter for me, and a strong tower from the enemy."

CONCLUSION: ". . . God shall supply all your need according to his riches in glory by Christ Jesus." Phil. 4:19. He will meet our every need. He is our Saviour, our sanctifier, our supplier and our security.

The God of Yesterday

Josh. 1:1-7

INTRODUCTION: "Moses is dead!" Joshua hears these words with a sinking heart. Anybody but Moses! He was worth a thousand men. Napoleon's men called him "OLD 200,000." Moses . . . Israel's Napoleon. *"MOSES IS DEAD!"* One of the world's greatest leaders. He was the one who saw the burning bush.

The one who went to Egypt alone, staff in hand. He fought with the hardhearted king and won. He was the one who led Israel out . . . brought water out of the rock . . . bread from heaven, etc. He had been everything to them. *He was a great man,* BUT, *now he is dead!*

I. LET US NOTICE FIRST, EVEN THOUGH IT WAS A GREAT CRUSHING BLOW, IT WAS NO TIME TO ASSUME AN ATTITUDE OF HOPELESSNESS.

    A. He was our leader, and was supposed to bring us to Canaan. *If he couldn't no one could!* No other among us is as great. Moses is dead. *Let's quit, give up* and *go back* to Egypt.

    B. This attitude is assumed by many today, when *the Moses of their lives dies.* One great defeat! A great sorrow came! One crushing disappointment! Life worthwhile no longer? No hope! We sit down and sob! We wait for the end. By so doing *we relegate God to yesterday. It CANNOT BE DONE . . . HE IS FOREVER THE "I AM." "FROM EVERLASTING TO EVERLASTING."* Heb. 13:8; Psa. 106:48.

II. THEY MIGHT HAVE REBELLED AND BECOME BITTER

    A. They might have blamed God . . . turned against

171

Him . . . gone back into Egypt. "MOSES DEAD!" We will quit. Never get anywhere without Moses. This is the fallacy of putting complete trust in any (1) man, (2) thing, (3) or any program.

B. No man or program is indispensable! God always has another personality and plan. God wouldn't have taken Moses to heaven if it would impede His work on earth. When *Elijah's term expired* God had Elisha. *God had already chosen and trained Joshua.*

C. Some think we need old-time preachers of 60 years ago today. NO! They were necessary in their day and God mightily used them. But maybe they wouldnt fit in today. God needs you and me. NO MAN IS INDISPENSABLE!
A bitter discouraged minister left a church and declared it would die. A new man came . . . new life came.

Another man quit his job at a factory. He went downhill, looked back. All lights were still on. The church will not die because a certain preacher leaves. The factory will not close down because a man quits. Thousands may die . . . thousands may leave . . . thousands may quit, but God's work will continue ever. Matt. 16:18.

D. A man went to a new pastorate. He followed a popular preacher. Members thought they must be disloyal to him to be loyal to the former pastor. One after another wanted transfers. Asked why, "Moses dead." Our beloved pastor is gone. Continued six weeks, then others wanted transfers.

He made a decision to give transfers to all who had requested them. He told the church the reason; he had seen a man open a bottled drink. It spurted and bubbled, but when all was over,

172

all lost was bubbles and wind. So he said, "All bubble and wind Christians step forward for transfers." No one came!

A man drained his pond because of the noise of the frogs. He drained it and found only two frogs.

Do not become disturbed because of a little complaining, murmuring, noise, etc. God can, and will, carry on His work. He keeps the stars in place, sends rain and sunshine without our help.

LESSONS TO LEARN FROM THIS INCIDENT

1. *GOD SPEAKS TO JOSHUA AFTER MOSES DIED.* "Now after the death of Moses . . . it came to pass, that the Lord spake unto Joshua." V. 1.

God did not quit speaking. *He spake after Moses died.* It is hard to believe. It is easy to believe He spake to Moses. He was a great man. But *Joshua, Moses' servant, was another matter.*

We must realize God spoke not only yesterday, but today as well. Heb. 13:8. He spoke to *great and mighty Moses,* and also to *common Joshua.*

2. *GOOD OLD DAYS? GONE? "MOSES IS DEAD!"*

True, God spoke to and directed our great men of the past, but equally true, God is still speaking to His own today.

3. *REAFFIRMS HIS PROMISE TO JOSHUA.* "Every place that the sole of your foot shall tread upon, that *have I given unto you,* as I said unto Moses." V. 3. Did not break (nor withdraw) His promise because *Moses died!*

173

Two things could have been done, God could have said, "I will make another (1) Moses out of Joshua, (2) God could have kept Moses." Joshua was not as big a man as Moses . . . never would have been . . . he did not need to be. (We all have our place . . . no one can do it all.) God can make man all he needs to be. *God is not limited,* to one day, one generation or one personality.

HIS PROMISE STILL STANDS . . . TO YOU . . . TO ME!

III. HE ASSURED JOSHUA OF HIS PRESENCE.

". . . as I was with Moses, so *I will be with thee!* I will not fail thee, nor forsake thee." Moses, the servant is dead *BUT* God, the Master, is not; He lives forever! "As I was with Moses" (1) *to direct him* so (2) to strengthen (3) to prosper.

Joshua knew he was not as great as Moses, but he also knew that if God was with him that would make him sufficient. What Moses did was because of God's presence and power.

He knew he was not like Moses. He did not try to be. *Moses could do a thousand things Joshua could not do,* but Joshua could *do something* Moses could not do. *He could do his own work, in his way,* as God gave him power; and that was enough. *In so doing, he entered Canaan. HE WON.*

IV. HE PROMISED JOSHUA SUCCESS

A. "There shall not any man . . . stand before thee all the 'days of thy life." V. 5.

B. God does not quit because one servant dies. He does not quit in the face of one failure. He calls another man, and His work continues. *HE MADE JOSHUA INVINCIBLE.* "No man

174

shall stand before thee." Promised victory over all foes. What more could one ask?

C. *Joshua could never be a Moses,* but he could and did have God's all-sufficiency.

D. *Finally, Moses is dead,* "now therefore, *arise, and go* over this Jordan, thou, and all this people."

Get up . . . arise . . . time to quit mourning . . . assume leadership . . . take these people over Jordan into Canaan. Impossible. Moses couldn't and I'm not near as mighty. Joshua, Moses is dead *BUT I AM ALIVE.*

When God finished speaking . . . JOSHUA TOOK COMMAND. He commanded the officers of the people saying. . . . V. 11.

V. ISRAEL'S REACTION TO HIS LEADERSHIP

A. OBEDIENCE. "All that thou commandest us we will do, and *whithersoever thou sendest us, we will go. According as we harkened unto Moses* in all things, so will we harken unto thee." VV. 16, 17.

B. PRAYER. ". . . only the Lord thy God be with thee, as he was with Moses." V. 17.

When God calls He equips us with anointing, power, influence and leadership.

MOSES IS DEAD . . . TRUE . . . BUT GOD LIVES!

Nearly 2,000 years ago when the sun had grown dark and all nature shuddered at the agony of a dying Saviour, God out of heaven cried, "My Son is dead. Arise and go." From that skull-shaped hill of loss and death, His followers went out to the conquest of the world.

Iniquity abounds. 2 Tim. 4:2-4; 1 Tim. 4:1;

Matt. 24:12. The church faces many discouragements today. Coldness, spiritual death, What should be our attitude? Give up? Take it easy? Quit? No! *ARISE AND GO ABOUT OUR FATHER'S BUSINESS.*

INDIVIDUAL LOSS: Some loved one passed away. Heart torn and bleeding. David and his child, good example. "He cannot return to me, but I can go to him."

John Bunyan locked in Bedford jail . . . no liberty . . . freedom . . . God's Word came to him. *"Moses is dead, arise and go."* Bunyan arose and went on a *preaching tour to the centuries.*

CONCLUSION: God's message to us today—*FORGET THE PAST—ARISE AND GO.*

"As I have spoken . . ."

"As I have given . . ."

"As I was with . . ."

"No man shall stand before thee . . ."

No failure need be final or fatal. Moses may die, but God lives on.

So, let us arise and take His hand and march triumphantly toward Canaan land.